The Hu

Devotional

Library of Congress Control Number:2019951724

Illustrations by Jessica Hagy

Interior design by Robaire Ream

ISBN: 9780988493865

The Humanist's Devotional

366 Daily Meditations from Some of the World's Greatest Thinkers

Jessica Hagy

Minneapolis–St. Paul

Introduction

Love > anger

fear < hope

optimism > despair

why you're holding this book

"My friends, love is better than anger.
Hope is better than fear. Optimism is
better than despair. So let us be loving,
hopeful and optimistic. And we'll change
the world."

—Jack Layton (WIKI)

This book interprets messages from 366 of our world's
most quoted and referenced thinkers.

It links them in a yearlong conversation that connects
ideas across cultures, eras, and topics. It gives you, every
day, an idea that will propel you forward.

Embrace your unknowns.

"When we try to pick out anything by itself we find that it is bound fast by a thousand invisible cords that cannot be broken, to everything in the universe."
—John Muir

"Everybody is ignorant, only on different subjects."
—Will Rogers

Admitting that you don't know something is the first step toward learning it.

Get excited about what's being discovered.

"Everybody is ignorant,
only on different subjects."
—Will Rogers

The depth of human knowledge grows every day.

"Nothing endures
but change."
—Heraclitus

Heed the radical voices.

"Nothing endures but change." —Heraclitus

All minds change over time.

"New opinions are always suspected, and usually opposed, without any other reason but because they are not already common."
—John Locke

Listen for emotion buried between chunks of jargon.

"New opinions are always suspected, and usually opposed, without any other reason but because they are not already common."
—John Locke

"The great enemy of clear language is insincerity."
—George Orwell

+

Speak more simply to be more widely understood.

Don't be ashamed of what you have accomplished.

"The great enemy of clear language is insincerity."
—George Orwell

Earned pride is nothing to be ashamed of.

"Show me someone not full of herself and I'll show you a hungry person."
—Nikki Giovanni

Know that nobody deserves everything they get.

"Show me someone not full of herself and I'll show you a hungry person."
—Nikki Giovanni

"Economics is all about how people make choices. Sociology is all about why they don't have any choices to make."
—James S. Duesenberry

Smugness is a side-effect of luck.

Give someone the benefit of your patience.

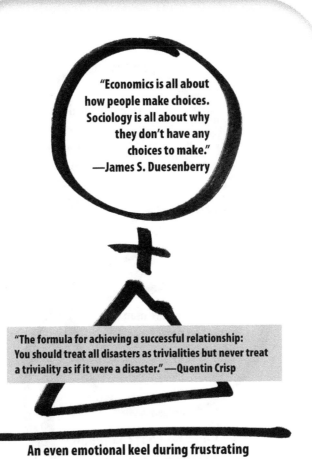

"Economics is all about how people make choices. Sociology is all about why they don't have any choices to make."
—James S. Duesenberry

"The formula for achieving a successful relationship: You should treat all disasters as trivialities but never treat a triviality as if it were a disaster." —Quentin Crisp

An even emotional keel during frustrating times can prevent many disasters.

Fail to air your petty grievances and you will forget them faster.

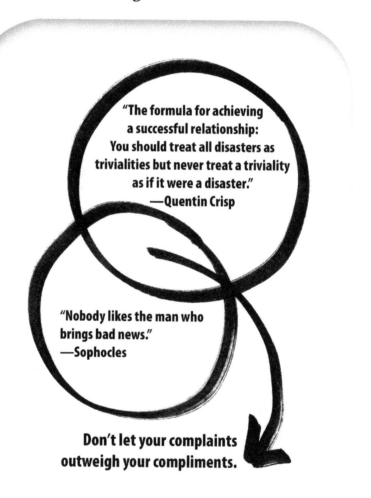

"The formula for achieving a successful relationship: You should treat all disasters as trivialities but never treat a triviality as if it were a disaster."
—Quentin Crisp

"Nobody likes the man who brings bad news."
—Sophocles

Don't let your complaints outweigh your compliments.

Never pick apart something harmless that makes people happy.

"Nobody likes the man who brings bad news."
—Sophocles

Gleefully punching holes in others' beliefs will make you unpopular.

**"Sacred cows make the tastiest hamburger."
—Abbie Hoffman**

Ask all the dumb questions you want.

"Sacred cows make the tastiest hamburger."
—Abbie Hoffman

Sudden realizations can make previously held ideas seem silly.

"How inappropriate to call this planet Earth when it is clearly Ocean."
—Arthur C. Clark

Revel in what captivates you.

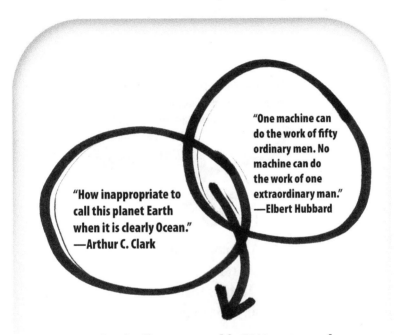

"How inappropriate to call this planet Earth when it is clearly Ocean."
—Arthur C. Clark

"One machine can do the work of fifty ordinary men. No machine can do the work of one extraordinary man."
—Elbert Hubbard

Our bodies are roughly 70% water and our potential is 100% imagination.

Let you mind wander to randomly fantastic places.

"One machine can do the work of fifty ordinary men. No machine can do the work of one extraordinary man."
—Elbert Hubbard

A curious mind can see further than any telescope.

"By convention there is color, by convention sweetness, by convention bitterness, but in reality there are atoms and space."
—Democritus

Notice something small and magnificent.

"By convention there is color, by convention sweetness, by convention bitterness, but in reality there are atoms and space."
—Democritus

"In all things of nature there is something of the marvelous."
—Aristotle

The closer you look, the less bored you'll feel.

Translate something assumed to be
dull into poetry.

"In all things of nature there is
something of the marvelous."
—Aristotle

Careful observation of our world leads to joy.

"The two foes of human
happiness are pain and boredom."
—Arthur Schopenhauer

Remind yourself that it's never really about you.

"The two foes of human happiness are pain and boredom."
—Arthur Schopenhauer

Not taking situations personally allows us to take them in stride.

"The universe is not hostile, nor is it friendly. It is simply indifferent."
—John Haynes Holmes

Be grateful for the many horrid things that didn't happen.

"We can never do merely one thing."
—Garrett Hardin

"The universe is not hostile, nor is it friendly. It is simply indifferent."
—John Haynes Holmes

Our every decision ripples out to infinite places we'll never visit.

Keep the children who won't be conceived for 300 years in mind.

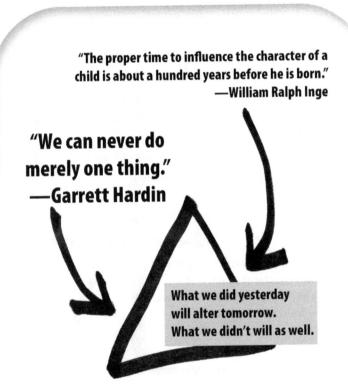

"The proper time to influence the character of a child is about a hundred years before he is born."
—William Ralph Inge

"We can never do merely one thing."
—Garrett Hardin

What we did yesterday will alter tomorrow. What we didn't will as well.

Be proud of what you've made with the circumstances you've been given.

"Gluttony is an emotional escape, a sign that something is eating us."
—Peter De Vries

"The proper time to influence the character of a child is about a hundred years before he is born."
—William Ralph Inge

We all metabolize our circumstances, and they make us who we are.

Try to parse the differences between your wants and needs.

"Gluttony is an emotional escape, a sign that something is eating us."
—Peter De Vries

Figuring out what we really need is an art form few ever perfect.

"Genius is nothing but a greater aptitude for patience."
—Georges-Louis Leclerc de Buffon

Unsubscribe and be merry.

"Genius is nothing but a greater
aptitude for patience."
—Georges-Louis Leclerc de Buffon

It's easier to use new inventions
than to realize they are using us.

"Only a free society can produce
technology that makes tyranny possible."
—John Keith Laumer

Accept that history books are propaganda.

"Only a free society can produce technology that makes tyranny possible."
—John Keith Laumer

The difference between a victim and a martyr can be seen in the eulogies given at her funeral.

"A man's dying is more the survivor's affair than his own."
—Thomas Mann

Do good work in a good person's memory.

"A man's dying is more the survivor's affair than his own." —Thomas Mann

You cannot rush the grieving process.

"Haste in every business brings failures." —Herodotus

Reach out to someone, not expecting a response.

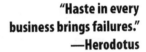

"Haste in every
business brings failures."
—Herodotus

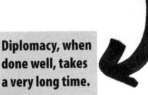

Diplomacy, when
done well, takes
a very long time.

"One murder makes a villain.
Millions, a hero."
—Beilby Porteus

Remember that everyone has a name and a dream.

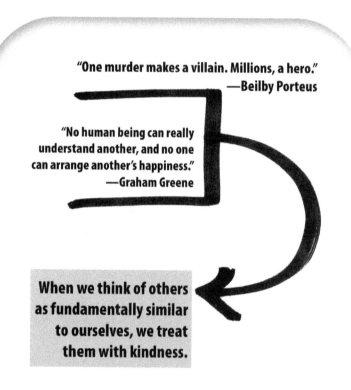

"One murder makes a villain. Millions, a hero."
—Beilby Porteus

"No human being can really understand another, and no one can arrange another's happiness."
—Graham Greene

When we think of others as fundamentally similar to ourselves, we treat them with kindness.

Tell someone you've never met
that you appreciate them.

"No human being can really understand
another, and no one can arrange
another's happiness."
—Graham Greene

We all want to be admired in our own, individual ways.

"A student never forgets
an encouraging private word
when it is given with sincere
respect and admiration."
—William Lyon Phelps

Accept feedback as proof you can do better.

"A student never forgets an encouraging private word when it is given with sincere respect and admiration."
—William Lyon Phelps

We learn who we are when other people compliment and criticize us.

"One can acquire everything in solitude—except character."
—Stendhal (Henri Beyle)

Arrange to meet up with the best people you know.

"One can acquire everything in solitude—except character."
—Stendhal (Henri Beyle)

We all secretly try to be as good as the best people we know.

"Sometimes I think the surest sign that intelligent life exists elsewhere in the universe is that none of it has tried to contact us."
—Bill Watterson

Read something scandalous.

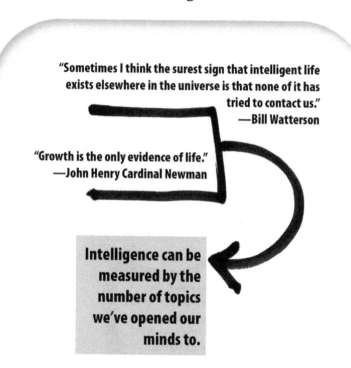

"Sometimes I think the surest sign that intelligent life exists elsewhere in the universe is that none of it has tried to contact us."
—Bill Watterson

"Growth is the only evidence of life."
—John Henry Cardinal Newman

Intelligence can be measured by the number of topics we've opened our minds to.

Be gentle with the kids who don't know any better.

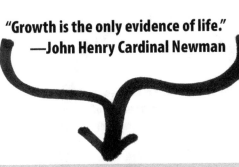

"Growth is the only evidence of life."
—John Henry Cardinal Newman

Every generation has to relearn everything its ancestors have already figured out.

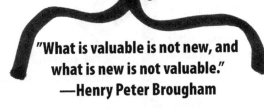

"What is valuable is not new, and what is new is not valuable."
—Henry Peter Brougham

Asking experts for insights helps you become one. Do that.

"What is valuable is not new, and what is new is not valuable."
—Henry Peter Brougham

"A dwarf standing on the shoulders of a giant may see farther than the giant himself."
—Robert Burton

When you think you've discovered a new world, you're wrong.
The people who already live there are the experts on that real estate.

Embark on a grand plan.

"A dwarf standing on the shoulders of a
giant may see farther than the giant himself."
—Robert Burton

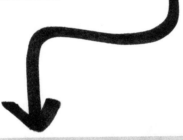

**Optimism without curiosity and
determination is simply wishful thinking.**

"The optimist proclaims that we live in the best of all
possible worlds; the pessimist fears this is true."
—James Branch Cabell

Avoid drama.

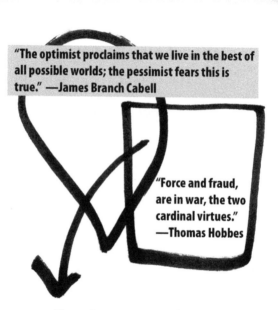

"The optimist proclaims that we live in the best of all possible worlds; the pessimist fears this is true." —James Branch Cabell

"Force and fraud, are in war, the two cardinal virtues." —Thomas Hobbes

If you have a sense that something isn't right, go somewhere better.

Look for goodness and you will find it.

"Force and fraud, are in war,
the two cardinal virtues."
—Thomas Hobbes

Be careful about how you
define what is worthwhile.

"We do not see things as they
are, but as we are ourselves."
—Henry M. Tomlinson

Try to project more kindness than insecurity.

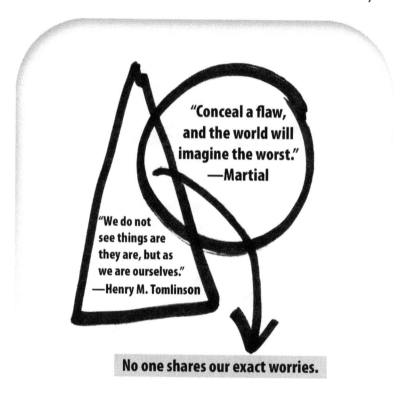

"Conceal a flaw,
and the world will
imagine the worst."
—Martial

"We do not
see things are
they are, but as
we are ourselves."
—Henry M. Tomlinson

No one shares our exact worries.

Don't hide behind filters.

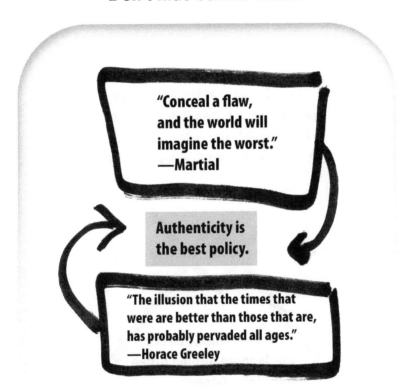

"Conceal a flaw,
and the world will
imagine the worst."
—Martial

Authenticity is
the best policy.

"The illusion that the times that
were are better than those that are,
has probably pervaded all ages."
—Horace Greeley

You will have accomplished more
by tomorrow.

"The illusion that the times that
were are better than those that are,
has probably pervaded all ages."
—Horace Greeley

You are always becoming more of who you are.

"A mathematician is a
machine for turning coffee
into theorems."
—Paul Erdos

Have hope that your work will pay off.

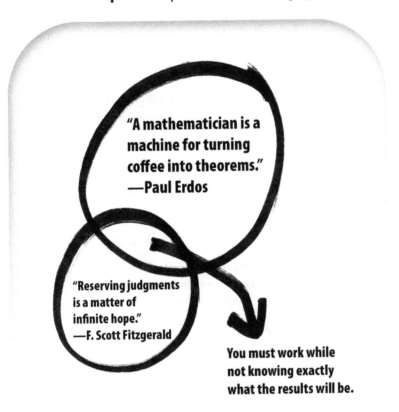

"A mathematician is a machine for turning coffee into theorems."
—Paul Erdos

"Reserving judgments is a matter of infinite hope."
—F. Scott Fitzgerald

You must work while not knowing exactly what the results will be.

You will surprise yourself if you
continue trying.

"Reserving judgments is
a matter of infinite hope."
—F. Scott Fitzgerald

What happens next
matters more than what
people think now.

"My interest is in the future
because I'm going to spend
the rest of my life there."
—Charles F. Kettering

Don't be discouraged by a bad day or several.

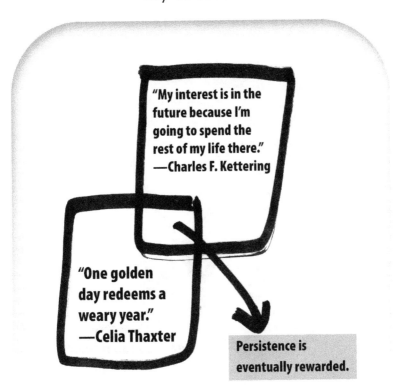

"My interest is in the future because I'm going to spend the rest of my life there."
—Charles F. Kettering

"One golden day redeems a weary year."
—Celia Thaxter

Persistence is eventually rewarded.

People will appreciate it when you overlook their flaws.

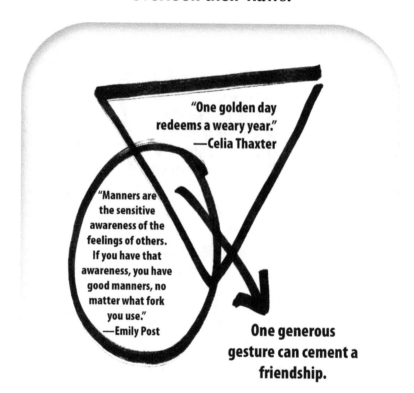

"One golden day redeems a weary year."
—Celia Thaxter

"Manners are the sensitive awareness of the feelings of others. If you have that awareness, you have good manners, no matter what fork you use."
—Emily Post

One generous gesture can cement a friendship.

You grow greater the more you overlook.

"Manners are the sensitive
awareness of the feelings of others.
If you have that awareness,
you have good manners,
no matter what fork you use."
—Emily Post

Give others the slack you wish you'd been granted.

"A friend is, as it were,
a second self."
—Cicero

An artist you love is a friend indeed.

"A friend is, as it were, a second self."
—Cicero

Let beautiful lyrics speak directly to you.

"Music has charms to soothe a savage breast, to soften rocks, or bend knotted oak."
—William Congreve

Listening always tells you something.

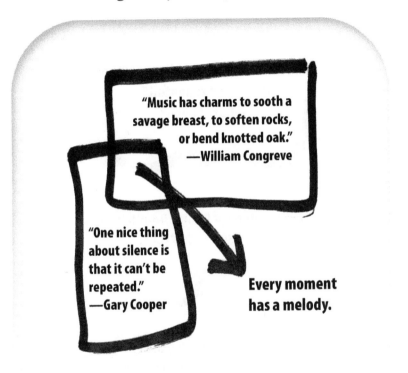

"Music has charms to sooth a savage breast, to soften rocks, or bend knotted oak."
—William Congreve

"One nice thing about silence is that it can't be repeated."
—Gary Cooper

Every moment has a melody.

Let go of old hang-ups.

"One nice thing about silence is that
it can't be repeated."
—Gary Cooper

**Moving forward means abandoning
old, useless crutches.**

"Insanity is doing the
same thing over and over again,
but expecting different results."
—Rita Mae Brown

Try something new with someone you were wary of.

"Insanity is doing the same thing over and over again, but expecting different results."
—Rita Mae Brown

Be open to the magic of other people's ideas.

"If you hate a person, you hate something in him that is part of yourself. What isn't part of ourselves doesn't disturb us."
—Hermann Hesse

Investigate thoroughly before constructing an opinion.

"If you hate a person, you hate something in him that is part of yourself.
What isn't part of ourselves doesn't disturb us."
—Hermann Hesse

"A book must be the ax for the frozen sea within us."
—Franz Kafka

You'll feel more if you dare to turn new pages.

Listen with an ear toward sympathy.

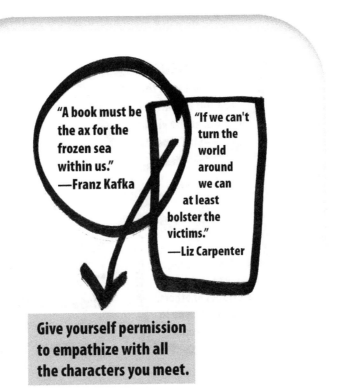

"A book must be the ax for the frozen sea within us."
—Franz Kafka

"If we can't turn the world around we can at least bolster the victims."
—Liz Carpenter

Give yourself permission to empathize with all the characters you meet.

Get closer to those who you usually ignore.

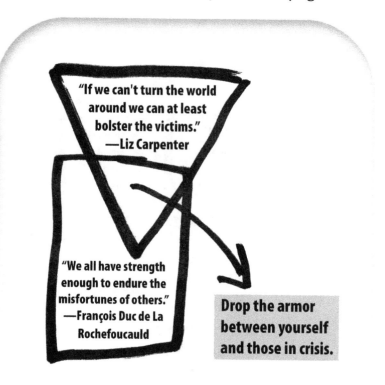

"If we can't turn the world around we can at least bolster the victims."
—Liz Carpenter

"We all have strength enough to endure the misfortunes of others."
—François Duc de La Rochefoucauld

Drop the armor between yourself and those in crisis.

Do not be afraid to step into
the hearts of others.

"We all have strength enough to
endure the misfortunes of others."
—François Duc de La Rochefoucauld

You'll know more if you
empathize more.

"Come forth into the light of things.
Let Nature be your teacher."
—William Wordsworth

Take care of someone else and you'll heal yourself.

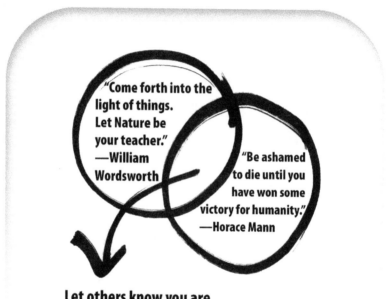

"Come forth into the light of things. Let Nature be your teacher."
—William Wordsworth

"Be ashamed to die until you have won some victory for humanity."
—Horace Mann

Let others know you are there to be of help.

Let your small, gentle gestures compile.

"Be ashamed to die until
you have won some victory
for humanity."
—Horace Mann

Even the smallest gift matters.

"No snowflake in
an avalanche ever
feels responsible."
—Stanislav J. Lec

Better to build your own momentum than be dragged along on someone else's wave.

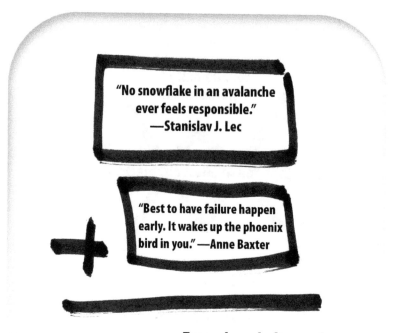

"No snowflake in an avalanche ever feels responsible."
—Stanislav J. Lec

"Best to have failure happen early. It wakes up the phoenix bird in you." —Anne Baxter

Try early and often and you will set your own course.

A nemesis can be a powerful motivator.

"Best to have failure
happen early. It wakes up the
phoenix bird in you."
—Anne Baxter

**Finding a way to let everyone win
is an awesome feat of navigation.**

"If you want to make peace,
you don't talk to your friends.
You talk to your enemies."
—Moshe Dayan

Do the dirty work first and the rest of your day better by default.

"If you want to make peace, you don't talk to your friends. You talk to your enemies."
—Moshe Dayan

"Literature is mostly about having sex and not much about having children. Life is the other way around."
—David Lodge

The chores you don't want to do are the tasks that most need doing.

Don't feel bad if your life is far from picture perfect.

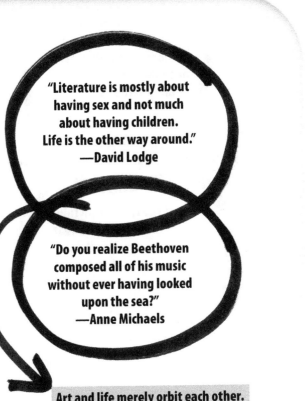

"Literature is mostly about having sex and not much about having children. Life is the other way around."
—David Lodge

"Do you realize Beethoven composed all of his music without ever having looked upon the sea?"
—Anne Michaels

Art and life merely orbit each other.

Deep feelings are powerful things.

"Do you realize Beethoven
composed all of his music
without ever having looked
upon the sea?"
—Anne Michaels

It's worthwhile to cry over what you've missed out on.

"The cure for anything
is saltwater: sweat,
tears, or the sea."
—Isak Dineson

**Extreme effort feels good even
if it yields no result.**

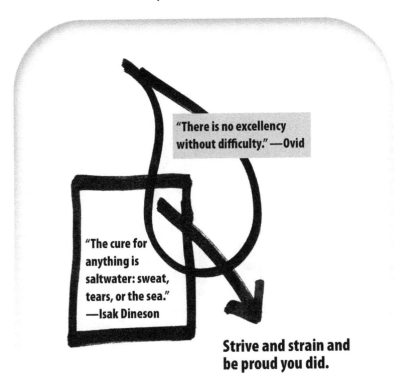

"There is no excellency
without difficulty." —Ovid

"The cure for
anything is
saltwater: sweat,
tears, or the sea."
—Isak Dineson

**Strive and strain and
be proud you did.**

Don't be afraid to begin.

"There is no excellency without difficulty."
—Ovid

The scariest things stop being that way once you tackle them.

"To get anywhere, strike out for somewhere, or you'll get nowhere."
—Martha Lupton

Define your destinations.

"To get anywhere, strike out for somewhere, or you'll get nowhere." —Martha Lupton

Chose an end point so you don't end up wandering in circles.

"Growth for the sake of growth is the ideology of the cancer cell." —Edward Abbey

Heroes plot more carefully than villains do.

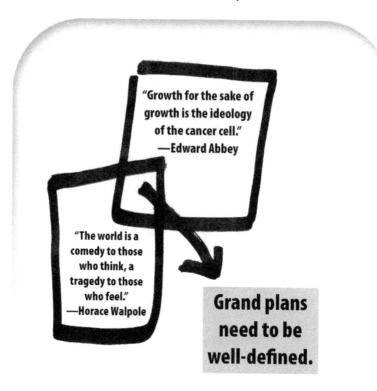

"Growth for the sake of growth is the ideology of the cancer cell."
—Edward Abbey

"The world is a comedy to those who think, a tragedy to those who feel."
—Horace Walpole

Grand plans need to be well-defined.

Do the math to see the truth.

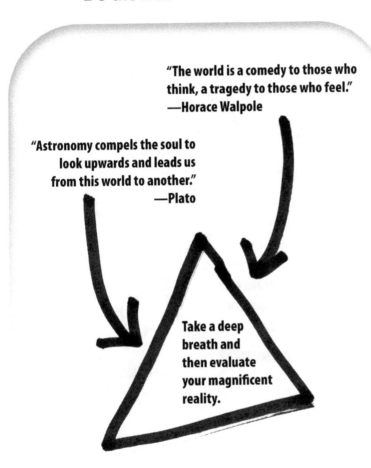

"The world is a comedy to those who think, a tragedy to those who feel."
—Horace Walpole

"Astronomy compels the soul to look upwards and leads us from this world to another."
—Plato

Take a deep breath and then evaluate your magnificent reality.

Research leads to clarity.

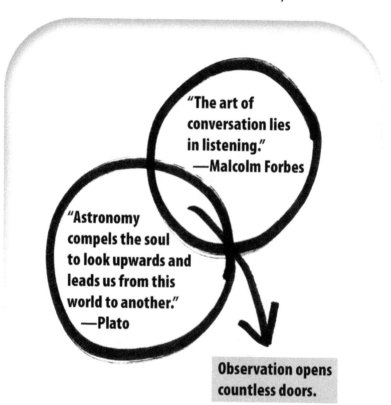

"The art of conversation lies in listening."
—Malcolm Forbes

"Astronomy compels the soul to look upwards and leads us from this world to another."
—Plato

Observation opens countless doors.

Let the experienced characters ramble.
You'll learn tons.

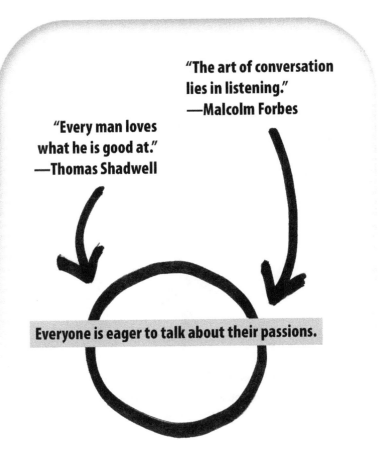

"The art of conversation
lies in listening."
—Malcolm Forbes

"Every man loves
what he is good at."
—Thomas Shadwell

Everyone is eager to talk about their passions.

It feels good to take concrete action.

"Every man loves what he is good at."
—Thomas Shadwell

**Making your agenda a reality
is deeply satisfying.**

"The value of a sentiment is the amount of
sacrifice you are prepared to make for it."
—John Galsworthy

Your actions will inspire others.

"The value of a sentiment is the amount of sacrifice you are prepared to make for it."
—John Galsworthy

Place yourself in difficult positions and you will learn how strong you really are.

"The mind is not a vessel to be filled but a fire to be kindled."
—Plutarch

Feed your brain quality material.

"Your imagination has much to do with your life. It pictures beauty, success, desired results. On the other hand, it brings into focus ugliness, distress, and failure. It is for you to decide how you want your imagination to serve you."
—Philip Conley

"The mind is not a vessel to be filled but a fire to be kindled."
—Plutarch

The best examples are those that make us say, "I can do that. Somehow."

Dive into obscure and beautiful media.

"Your imagination has much to do with your life.
It pictures beauty, success, desired results.
On the other hand, it brings into focus ugliness,
distress, and failure. It is for you to decide how
you want your imagination to serve you."
—Philip Conley

If you only read what everyone else does,
you'll only think how everyone else does.

"If 50 million people
say a foolish thing,
it is still a foolish thing."
—Anatole France

Don't worry what other people
think of you now.

"If 50 million people say a foolish
thing, it is still a foolish thing."
—Anatole France

"Every society honors its live
conformists, and its dead
troublemakers."
—Mignon McLaughlin

Dare to say things that won't
be common sense for decades.

Speak the truth and have no fear.

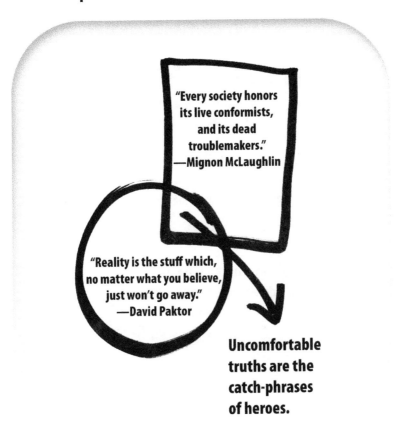

"Every society honors its live conformists, and its dead troublemakers."
—Mignon McLaughlin

"Reality is the stuff which, no matter what you believe, just won't go away."
—David Paktor

Uncomfortable truths are the catch-phrases of heroes.

Our shared, real world is a fascinating place.

"Reality is the stuff which, no matter what you believe, just won't go away." —David Paktor

Reality can be more captivating than fantasy, if you let it be.

"Intellectual passion drives out sensuality."
—Leonardo da Vinci

Note the power of the well-chosen
language you hear.

"Intellectual passion drives
out sensuality."
—Leonardo da Vinci

Words are only stand-ins for pieces of reality.

"A sharp tongue is the only
edged tool that grows
keener with constant use."
—Washington Irving

What you say can redefine who you are.

"A sharp tongue is the only edged tool
that grows keener with constant use."
—Washington Irving

Language is a
form of fashion.

"Every man's work, whether it be literature
or music or pictures or architecture or anything
else, is always a portrait of himself."
—Samuel Butler

Know your audiences.

"Every man's work, whether it be literature or music or pictures or architecture or anything else, is always a portrait of himself."
—Samuel Butler

It's amazing how many friends one well-phrased thought can make.

"A difference in taste in jokes is a great strain on the affections."
—George Elliot (Mary Ann Evans)

**There are a thousand ways
to say a single thing.**

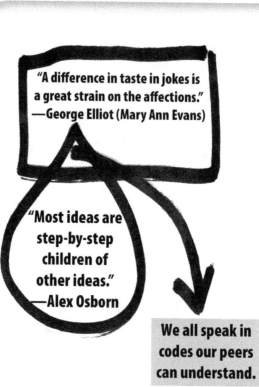

"A difference in taste in jokes is
a great strain on the affections."
—George Elliot (Mary Ann Evans)

"Most ideas are
step-by-step
children of
other ideas."
—Alex Osborn

We all speak in
codes our peers
can understand.

Focus on your strengths, but augment them with bits of everything else.

"Most ideas are step-by-step children of other ideas."
—Alex Osborn

You must borrow a thousand ideas to make one thing all your own.

"We are not all capable of everything."
—Sallust

It's okay to be ignorant sometimes.

"We are not all
capable of everything."
—Sallust

"Information is not power.
If information were power, then
librarians would be the most powerful
people on the planet."
—Bruce Sterling

**Focus on what you can do instead
of what you do not know.**

Gather resources before taking action.

"Information is not power. If information were power, then librarians would be the most powerful people on the planet."
—Bruce Sterling

"Anger is a prelude to courage."
—Eric Hoffer

Knowing enough to be dangerous is a great feeling.

The more certain you are about it, the more people will help you with it.

"Anger is a prelude to courage."
—Eric Hoffer

"A leader is a dealer in hope."
—Napoleon Bonaparte

If you're brave enough, others will feel the same way.

A leader without followers is no leader at all.

"A leader is a dealer in hope."
—Napoleon Bonaparte

Believe in something big enough that people want to be a part of it.

"What do we live for, if it is not to make life less difficult for each other?"
—George Eliot

Aim high, then help others up the ladder behind you.

"What do we live for,
if it is not to make life less
difficult for each other?"
—George Eliot

A winning movement promises more to all who join it.

"One can never consent to
creep when one feels the
impulse to soar."
—Helen Keller

Highs and lows come in waves.

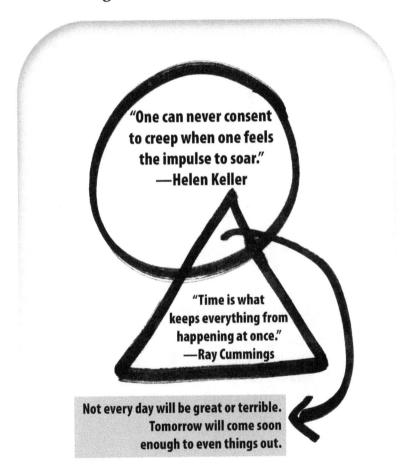

"One can never consent
to creep when one feels
the impulse to soar."
—Helen Keller

"Time is what
keeps everything from
happening at once."
—Ray Cummings

Not every day will be great or terrible.
Tomorrow will come soon
enough to even things out.

Plan for what you want.

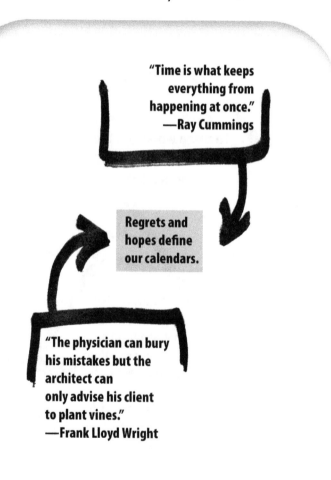

"Time is what keeps everything from happening at once."
—Ray Cummings

Regrets and hopes define our calendars.

"The physician can bury his mistakes but the architect can only advise his client to plant vines."
—Frank Lloyd Wright

Wins are sweeter if losses are understood.

"The physician can bury his mistakes but the architect can only advise his client to plant vines."
—Frank Lloyd Wright

Our successes and failures are context for the other.

"A little alarm now and then keeps life from stagnation."
—Fanny Burney

Excitement fractures routines.

"A little alarm now and then keeps life from stagnation."
—Fanny Burney

Chaos is more stimulating than being stuck in a rut.

"Habit is thus the enormous fly-wheel of society, its most precious conservative agent. It alone is what keeps us all within the bounds of ordinance." —William James

Change your life by breaking from convention.

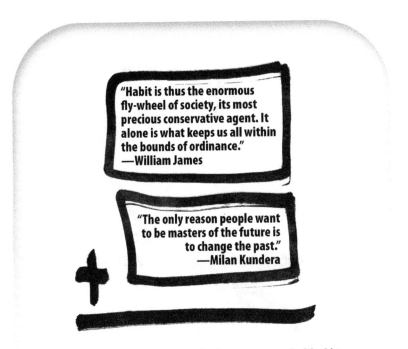

"Habit is thus the enormous fly-wheel of society, its most precious conservative agent. It alone is what keeps us all within the bounds of ordinance."
—William James

"The only reason people want to be masters of the future is to change the past."
—Milan Kundera

Today's boredom has yesterday's momentum behind it.

Specialize to affect the future.

"The only reason people want to be masters of the future is to change the past."
—Milan Kundera

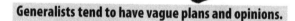

Generalists tend to have vague plans and opinions.

"A specialist is a man who knows more and more about less and less."
—William J. Mayo

Plan for far later and it will be far better.

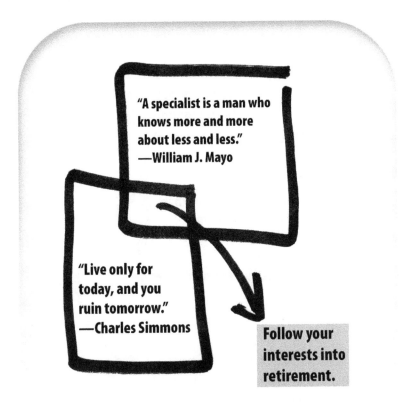

"A specialist is a man who knows more and more about less and less."
—William J. Mayo

"Live only for today, and you ruin tomorrow."
—Charles Simmons

Follow your interests into retirement.

Do as your heroes would.

"Live only for today,
and you ruin tomorrow."
—Charles Simmons

"People never improve unless they
look to some standard or some
example higher than themselves."
—Tyron Edwards

Aim to be a part of
something monumental
and you'll leave a legacy.

You'll never regret not giving up.

"People never improve unless
they look to some standard
or some example higher
than themselves."
—Tyron Edwards

You'll forget how hard it was to reach your goal after you do.

"Time cancels
young pain."
—Euripides

What you do defines who you are.

"Time cancels
young pain."
—Euripides

When in doubt,
be of comfort.

"The gentle mind by gentle deeds
is known. For a man by nothing
is so well betrayed, as by his manners."
—Edmund Spencer

Not all successes have to be complicated.

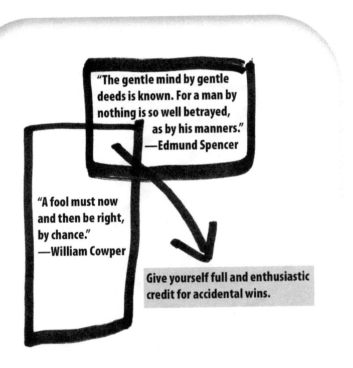

"The gentle mind by gentle deeds is known. For a man by nothing is so well betrayed, as by his manners."
—Edmund Spencer

"A fool must now and then be right, by chance."
—William Cowper

Give yourself full and enthusiastic credit for accidental wins.

Accept that brilliance is often fleeting.

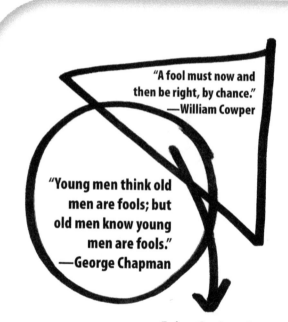

"A fool must now and then be right, by chance."
—William Cowper

"Young men think old men are fools; but old men know young men are fools."
—George Chapman

Enjoy the fact that we're all dumb and wise at different times.

Give yourself enough slack not to burn out.

"Young men think old men are fools; but old men know young men are fools."
—George Chapman

"Be charitable and indulgent to everyone but yourself."
—Joseph Joubert

Forgive others quickly but keep yourself on task.

Your hard work is only a fraction
of why you'll succeed.

"Be charitable and
indulgent to everyone
but yourself."
—Joseph Joubert

Nobody gets anywhere impressive alone.

"Too many of us, when we
accomplish what we've set
out to do, exclaim, "See what
I've done!" instead of saying,
"See where I've been led.""
—Henry Ford

Every large accomplishment was shaped by many minor setbacks.

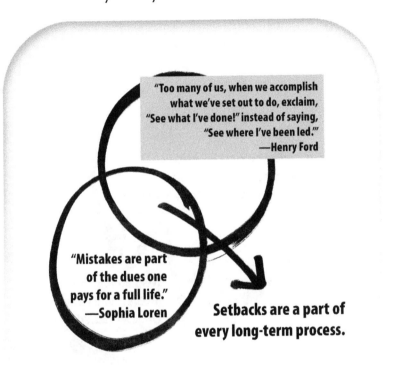

"Too many of us, when we accomplish what we've set out to do, exclaim, "See what I've done!" instead of saying, "See where I've been led."'
—Henry Ford

"Mistakes are part of the dues one pays for a full life."
—Sophia Loren

Setbacks are a part of every long-term process.

The benefit of the doubt is a gift.

"Mistakes are part of the dues
one pays for a full life."
—Sophia Loren

"In this world, you must be a bit
too kind in order to be kind enough."
—Pierre Carlet de Chamblain de Marivaux

Work around the
problem and forgive
whoever caused it.

Share what you know.

"In this world, you must be a bit too kind in order to be kind enough."
—Pierre Carlet de Chamblain de Marivaux

"Diffused knowledge immortalizes itself."
—Sir James Mackintosh

Be generous with your skills, and they'll do more than you alone ever could.

Information shared is information in action.

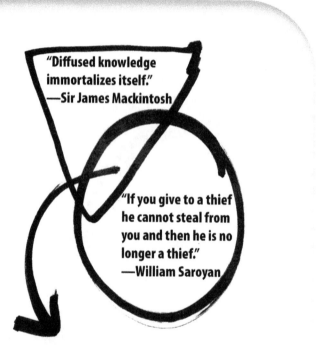

"Diffused knowledge immortalizes itself."
—Sir James Mackintosh

"If you give to a thief he cannot steal from you and then he is no longer a thief."
—William Saroyan

You can change an entire life with one helpful gesture.

Know the difference between valuable
information and annoying advice.

"If you give to a thief he cannot steal
from you and then he is no longer a thief."
—William Saroyan

Only give advice if it's asked for.

"Too bad all the people who know
how to run the country are busy
driving taxi cabs and cutting hair."
—George Burns

Ordinary people know more than they're given credit for.

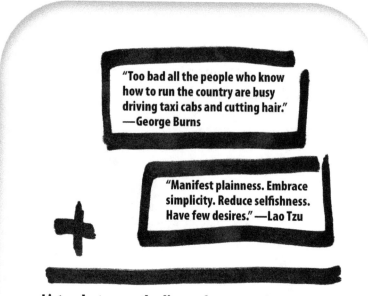

"Too bad all the people who know how to run the country are busy driving taxi cabs and cutting hair."
—George Burns

"Manifest plainness. Embrace simplicity. Reduce selfishness. Have few desires." —Lao Tzu

Listen between the lines of a rant to hear wisdom.

Give away something of value.

"Manifest plainness.
Embrace simplicity.
Reduce selfishness.
Have few desires."
—Lao Tzu

"That action is best which
procures the greatest happiness
for the greatest numbers."
—Francis Hutcheson

**Simplicity
conjures
happiness.**

Spend time in nature. You'll feel smaller and larger at once.

"That action is best which procures the greatest happiness for the greatest numbers."
—Francis Hutcheson

Protect a vista and you protect the town below it.

"Mountains are earth's decaying monuments."
—Nathaniel Hawthorne

Trust science that's not stamped with a logo.

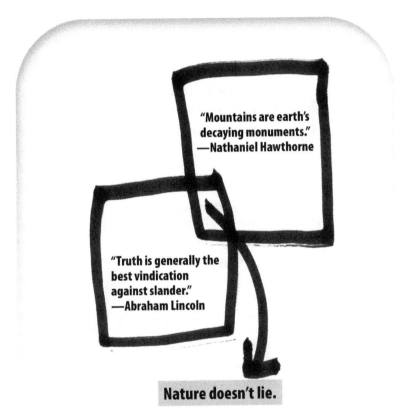

"Mountains are earth's decaying monuments."
—Nathaniel Hawthorne

"Truth is generally the best vindication against slander."
—Abraham Lincoln

Nature doesn't lie.

Know that even nasty people can teach you something.

"Truth is generally the best vindication against slander."
—Abraham Lincoln

Every time you encounter malice, you'll better know what to avoid next time.

"If you can't be a good example, then you'll just have to be a horrible warning."
—Catherine Aird

Remember that everyone is mostly doing their best.

"If you can't be a good example,
then you'll just have to be
a horrible warning."
—Catherine Aird

There's a criminal who should be forgiven inside all of us.

"Where all, or almost all,
are guilty, nobody is."
—Hannah Arendt

Give yourself permission to use the loopholes available.

"Where all, or almost all, are guilty, nobody is."
—Hannah Arendt

"Chaos often breeds life, when order breeds habit."
—Henry Brooks Adams

Being too rigid about rules means the dumb ones get enforced.

Let everybody be a little weird.

"Chaos often breeds life,
when order breeds habit."
—Henry Brooks Adams

Taking offense at slightly deviant
behaviors is a method of
mandating conformity.

"Intolerance of groups is
often, strangely enough,
exhibited more strongly
against small differences than
against fundamental ones."
—Sigmund Freud

It's our differences that keep life interesting.

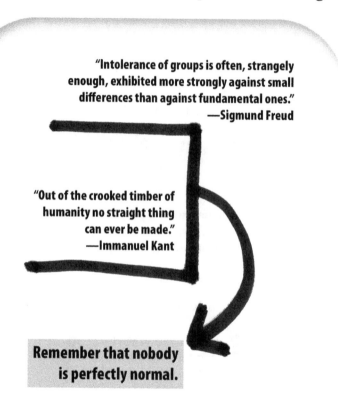

"Intolerance of groups is often, strangely enough, exhibited more strongly against small differences than against fundamental ones."
—Sigmund Freud

"Out of the crooked timber of humanity no straight thing can ever be made."
—Immanuel Kant

Remember that nobody is perfectly normal.

Approach all work like it's an art project.
Messes are discoveries.

"Out of the crooked
timber of humanity
no straight thing
can ever be made."
—Immanuel Kant

Go where your experiments take you, not
where you wish they would lead.

"Fanaticism consists in redoubling
your effort when you have
forgotten your aim."
—George Santayana

Work is better if it means something to you.

"Fanaticism consists in redoubling your effort when you have forgotten your aim."
—George Santayana

Never forget why you're doing what you're doing.

"I feel the greatest reward for doing is the opportunity to do more."
—Jonas Salk

If one project fails, there will always be others.

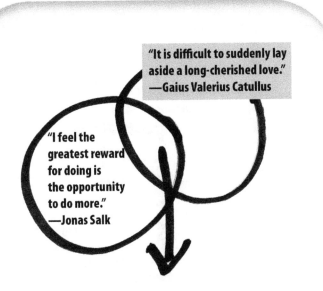

"It is difficult to suddenly lay aside a long-cherished love."
—Gaius Valerius Catullus

"I feel the greatest reward for doing is the opportunity to do more."
—Jonas Salk

Pink slips are open doors.

End relationships with kind words.

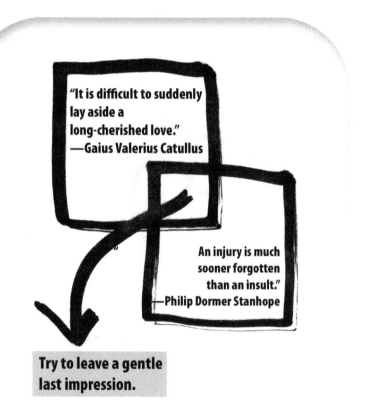

"It is difficult to suddenly lay aside a long-cherished love."
—Gaius Valerius Catullus

An injury is much sooner forgotten than an insult."
—Philip Dormer Stanhope

Try to leave a gentle last impression.

Don't read the comments.

"An injury is much sooner
forgotten than an insult."
—Philip Dormer Stanhope

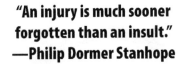

One cruel statement
can undo a
thousand compliments.

"The things we remember best
are those best forgotten."
—Baltasar Gracian

If you're feeling low, bond with others over things you've done together.

"The things we remember best are those best forgotten."
—Baltasar Gracian

"The best ideas are common property."
—Seneca

Accomplishments get shared while failures feel personal.

Make your compliments specific and personal.

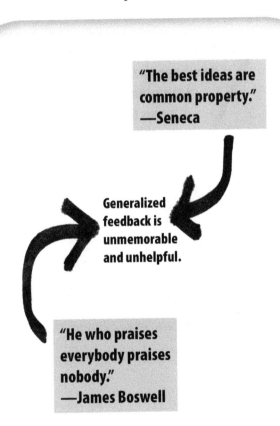

"The best ideas are common property."
—Seneca

Generalized feedback is unmemorable and unhelpful.

"He who praises everybody praises nobody."
—James Boswell

No single purchase can change your life.

"He who praises everybody praises nobody."
—James Boswell

Doubt paid spokespeople.

"You can tell the ideals of a nation by its advertisements."
—Norman Douglas

The best things are things that capture our imagination.

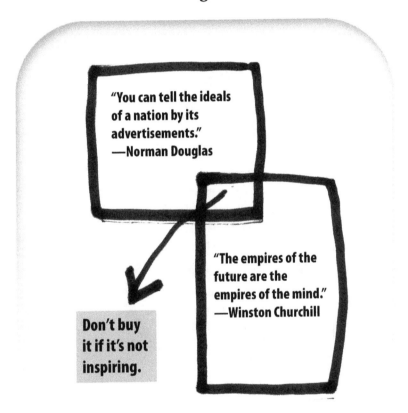

"You can tell the ideals of a nation by its advertisements."
—Norman Douglas

"The empires of the future are the empires of the mind."
—Winston Churchill

Don't buy it if it's not inspiring.

Make room in your brain for
fantastic possibility.

"The empires
of the future
are the empires
of the mind."
—Winston Churchill

Indulging in fiction can make the real world more magical.

"A myth is a religion in which
no-one any longer believes."
—James K. Feibleman

Put more faith in workers than CEOs.

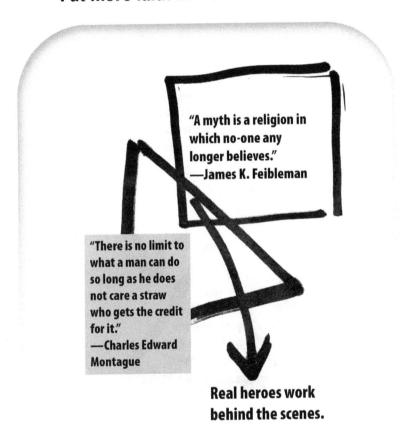

"A myth is a religion in which no-one any longer believes."
—James K. Feibleman

"There is no limit to what a man can do so long as he does not care a straw who gets the credit for it."
—Charles Edward Montague

Real heroes work behind the scenes.

If you are told, "No," by a boss, then work outside the hierarchy.

"There is no limit to what a man can do so long as he does not care a straw who gets the credit for it."
—Charles Edward Montague

"You have not converted a man because you have silenced him."
—John Morley

Work outside the spotlight is the work that will change the world.

People hide shunned behaviors.

"You have not converted a man
because you have silenced him."
—John Morley

Just because you don't see it doesn't
mean it's not happening.

"Reality is a crutch for people
who can't cope with drugs."
—Jane Wagner

May 1

Everything is amazing if you can
piece it together.

"Reality is a crutch for
people who can't
cope with drugs."
—Jane Wagner

"Creative thinking will
improve as we relate the
new fact to the old and
all facts to each other."
—John Dewey

If you want to blow your mind
frequently, read new things constantly.

Every person knows something that's helpful to someone else.

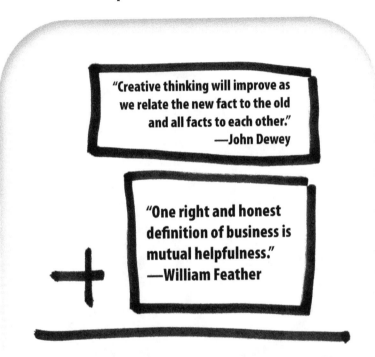

"Creative thinking will improve as we relate the new fact to the old and all facts to each other."
—John Dewey

"One right and honest definition of business is mutual helpfulness."
—William Feather

Your ideas can make someone else's come to life.

Nothing makes money unless it solves a human problem.

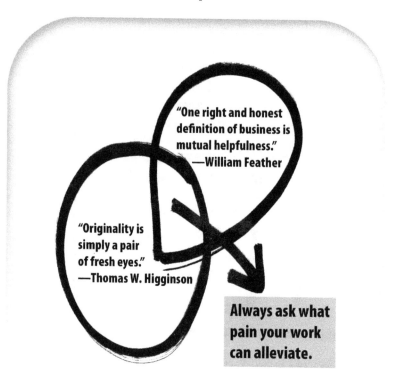

"One right and honest definition of business is mutual helpfulness."
—William Feather

"Originality is simply a pair of fresh eyes."
—Thomas W. Higginson

Always ask what pain your work can alleviate.

Novelties grow stale when they get popular.

"Originality is simply
a pair of fresh eyes."
—Thomas W. Higginson

The next big thing is an evolution of what came before it.

"The free thinking of
one age is the common
sense of the next."
—Matthew Arnold

**Learn the basics before attempting
to innovate.**

"The free thinking of
one age is the common
sense of the next."
—Matthew Arnold

"So long as the
mother, Ignorance,
lives, it is not safe for
Science, the offspring,
to divulge the
hidden causes of things."
—Johannes Kepler

The best ideas
are built on solid
intellectual
foundations.

**It's impossible to be an expert
on everything.**

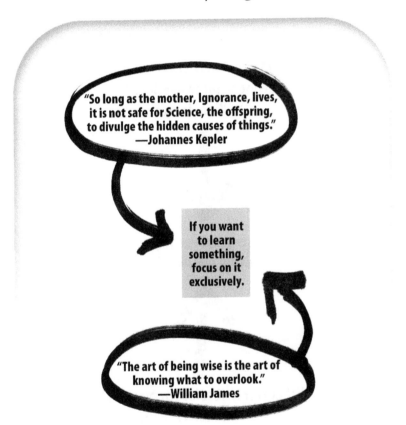

"So long as the mother, Ignorance, lives,
it is not safe for Science, the offspring,
to divulge the hidden causes of things."
—Johannes Kepler

If you want
to learn
something,
focus on it
exclusively.

"The art of being wise is the art of
knowing what to overlook."
—William James

Ignore human foibles and you'll keep
the peace.

"The art of being wise is the art of
knowing what to overlook."
—William James

Dumb actions are
often violent.

"Either war is obsolete or men are."
—R. Buckminster Fuller

Anger leads to terrible messes.

"Long after the bomb falls and you and your good deeds are gone, cockroaches will still be here, prowling the streets like armored cars."
—Tama Janowitz

"Either war is obsolete or men are."
—R. Buckminster Fuller

No argument is worth a scorched-earth response.

We must make the best of our imperfect situations.

"Long after the bomb falls and you and your good deeds are gone, cockroaches will still be here, prowling the streets like armored cars."
—Tama Janowitz

At the end of every catastrophe, we have to dust ourselves off and keep going.

"I was a victim of a series of accidents, as are we all."
—Kurt Vonnegut, Jr.

Your chosen people will help you through anything.

"I was a victim of a series of accidents, as are we all."
—Kurt Vonnegut, Jr.

Find people who relate to you, even if they're not related to you.

"Call it a clan, call it a network, call it a tribe, call it a family. Whatever you call it, whoever you are, you need one."
—Jane Howard

We all play many roles for each other.

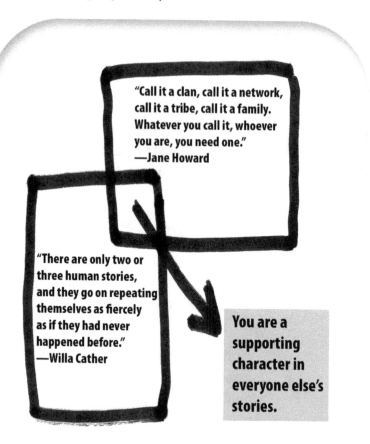

"Call it a clan, call it a network, call it a tribe, call it a family. Whatever you call it, whoever you are, you need one."
—Jane Howard

"There are only two or three human stories, and they go on repeating themselves as fiercely as if they had never happened before."
—Willa Cather

You are a supporting character in everyone else's stories.

You've inherited more than you realize.

"There are only two or three human stories,
and they go on repeating themselves as fiercely
as if they had never happened before."
—Willa Cather

Today's not entirely your fault,
but it is entirely your problem.

"The secret of great fortunes without
apparent source is forgotten crime."
—Honoré de Balzac

Victory does not equal valor.

"The secret of great
fortunes without apparent
source is forgotten crime."
—Honoré de Balzac

Choose your heroes wisely.

"The greatest minds are
capable of the greatest
vices as well as the
greatest virtues."
—René Descartes

Be gentle with the power you possess.

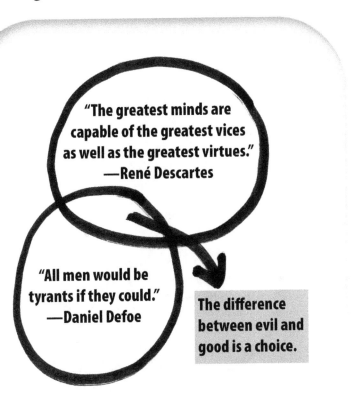

"The greatest minds are capable of the greatest vices as well as the greatest virtues."
—René Descartes

"All men would be tyrants if they could."
—Daniel Defoe

The difference between evil and good is a choice.

Comparing yourself to all others will always depress you.

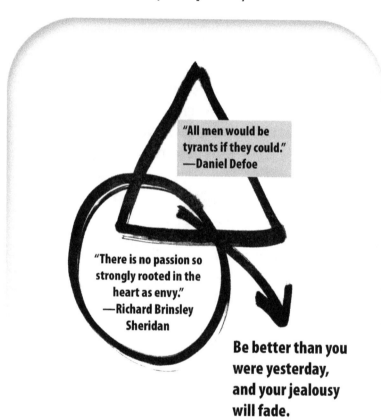

"All men would be tyrants if they could."
—Daniel Defoe

"There is no passion so strongly rooted in the heart as envy."
—Richard Brinsley Sheridan

Be better than you were yesterday, and your jealousy will fade.

Do good work and the praise will follow.

"There is no passion so strongly rooted in the heart as envy."
—Richard Brinsley Sheridan

"One must be something in order to do something."
—Johann Wolfgang von Goethe

Aim for mastery, not popularity.

We all have vastly different goals.

"One must be something
in order to do something."
—Johann Wolfgang von Goethe

"No human being
can really understand
another, and no one can
arrange another's happiness."
—Graham Greene

Very few people want to
be you when they grow up.
Don't take offense.
You don't want to be them, either.

Give people space to be themselves.

"No human being can really understand another,
and no one can arrange another's happiness."
—Graham Greene

What you do alone in a
room reveals your truest self.

"Architecture is inhabited sculpture."
—Constantin Brancusi

Your home is a political result.

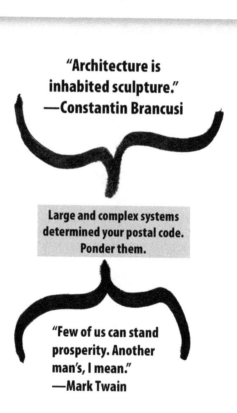

"Architecture is
inhabited sculpture."
—Constantin Brancusi

Large and complex systems
determined your postal code.
Ponder them.

"Few of us can stand
prosperity. Another
man's, I mean."
—Mark Twain

Put your money where your ideals are.

"Few of us can stand prosperity. Another man's, I mean."
—Mark Twain

"Words without actions are the assassins of idealism."
—Herbert Hoover

Mere venting won't change anyone's life.

In and out of the newspaper news
matters more than opinions.

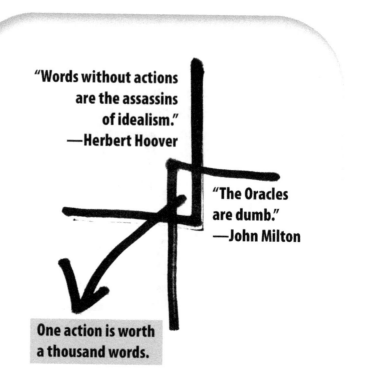

"Words without actions
are the assassins
of idealism."
—Herbert Hoover

"The Oracles
are dumb."
—John Milton

One action is worth
a thousand words.

Not having an opinion is an opinion.

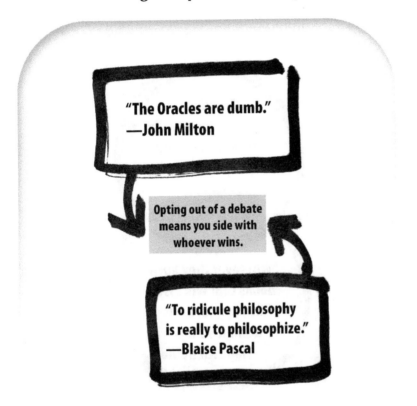

"The Oracles are dumb."
—John Milton

Opting out of a debate means you side with whoever wins.

"To ridicule philosophy is really to philosophize."
—Blaise Pascal

Ideas are the strength of humanity.

"To ridicule philosophy is really to philosophize."
—Blaise Pascal

Uncurious minds are the most dangerous.

"Wherever they burn books that will also, in the end, burn human beings."
—Heinrich Heine

The worst idea is refusing to have some.

"Wherever they burn books that will
also, in the end, burn human beings."
—Heinrich Heine

"The whole secret of the study of nature
lies in learning how to use one's eyes."
—George Sand

Paying attention is advantageous to survival.

Notice who takes credit for what.

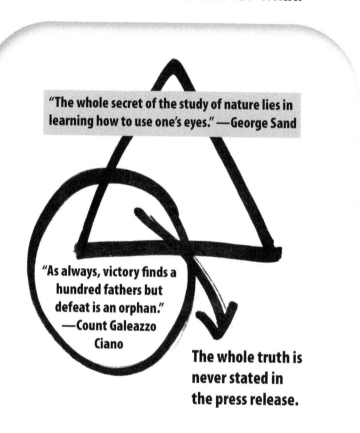

"The whole secret of the study of nature lies in learning how to use one's eyes." —George Sand

"As always, victory finds a hundred fathers but defeat is an orphan." —Count Galeazzo Ciano

The whole truth is never stated in the press release.

Effects are explained by their assumed causes.

"As always, victory finds a
hundred fathers but
defeat is an orphan."
—Count Galeazzo Ciano

All ancestry references are metaphors.

"Variety is the mother
of enjoyment."
—Benjamin Disraeli

Your ancestors are a motley crew.

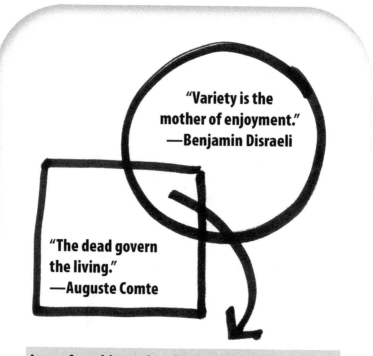

"Variety is the
mother of enjoyment."
—Benjamin Disraeli

"The dead govern
the living."
—Auguste Comte

Learn from history but don't let it limit the future.

You can change the future by what
you do today.

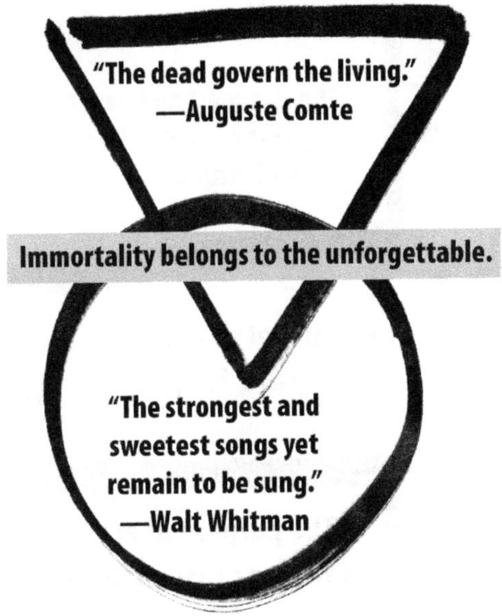

"The dead govern the living."
—Auguste Comte

Immortality belongs to the unforgettable.

"The strongest and
sweetest songs yet
remain to be sung."
—Walt Whitman

There are masterpieces inside you,
waiting to be built.

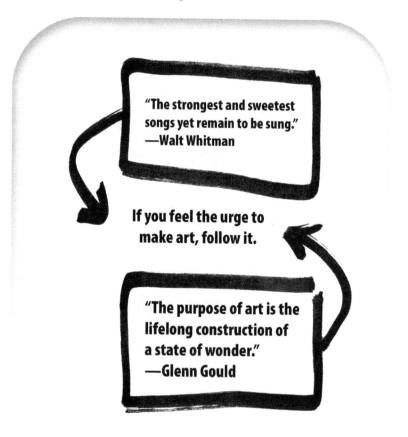

"The strongest and sweetest
songs yet remain to be sung."
—Walt Whitman

If you feel the urge to
make art, follow it.

"The purpose of art is the
lifelong construction of
a state of wonder."
—Glenn Gould

Better to be amazed than be at ease.

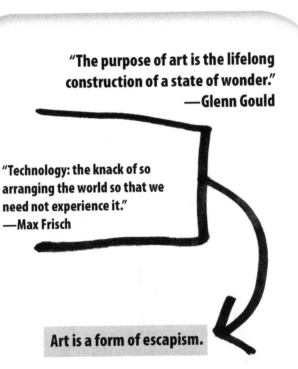

"The purpose of art is the lifelong construction of a state of wonder."
—Glenn Gould

"Technology: the knack of so arranging the world so that we need not experience it."
—Max Frisch

Art is a form of escapism.

Your abilities should make your life richer, not more boring.

"Technology: the knack of so arranging the world so that we need not experience it."
—Max Frisch

To truly engage we must frequently unplug.

"Everyone has talent. What is rare is the courage to follow the talent to the dark place where it leads."
—Erica Jong

Strive to trigger gasps, not shrugs.

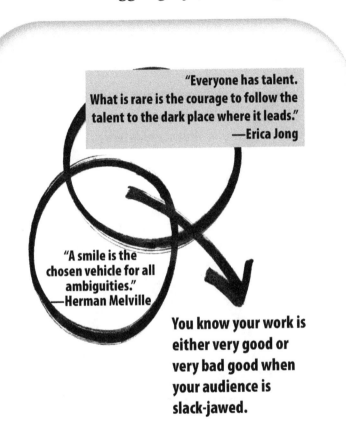

"Everyone has talent. What is rare is the courage to follow the talent to the dark place where it leads."
—Erica Jong

"A smile is the chosen vehicle for all ambiguities."
—Herman Melville

You know your work is either very good or very bad good when your audience is slack-jawed.

Plant a tree and everyone can breathe
more deeply.

"A smile is the chosen vehicle
for all ambiguities."
—Herman Melville

"Oh well," is not a valid answer to oncoming catastrophe.

"A thing is right when it tends to
preserve the integrity, stability,
and beauty of the biotic community.
It is wrong when it tends otherwise."
—Aldo Leopold

Don't buy trash.

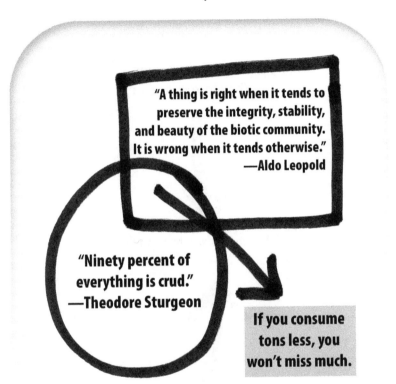

"A thing is right when it tends to preserve the integrity, stability, and beauty of the biotic community. It is wrong when it tends otherwise."
—Aldo Leopold

"Ninety percent of everything is crud."
—Theodore Sturgeon

If you consume tons less, you won't miss much.

Look to the greats for inspiration.

"Ninety percent of everything is crud."
—Theodore Sturgeon

Don't let mediocrity inform your work.
You can only do better if you see better.

"The marble not yet carved can hold the form of
every thought the greatest artist has."
—Michelangelo

Look for the potential inside every material.

"The marble not yet carved can
hold the form of every thought
the greatest artist has."
—Michelangelo

It's human a gift to be able to imagine.

"There is a passion for hunting
something deeply implanted
in the human breast."
—Charles Dickens

Spend your money on your soul.

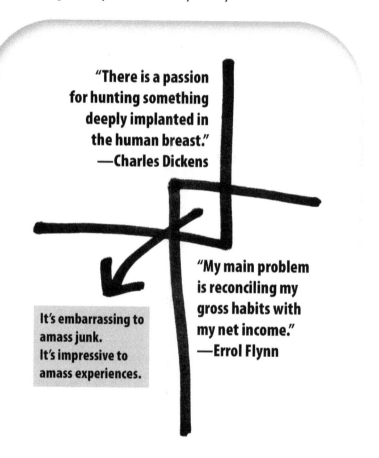

"There is a passion
for hunting something
deeply implanted in
the human breast."
—Charles Dickens

"My main problem
is reconciling my
gross habits with
my net income."
—Errol Flynn

It's embarrassing to
amass junk.
It's impressive to
amass experiences.

Decide what your money is for.

"My main problem is reconciling my gross habits with my net income."
—Errol Flynn

Money is only one variable in the equation of life.

"To be smart enough to get all that money you must be dull enough to want it."
—G. K. Chesterton

Use what you have or it will rust.

"To be smart enough to get all that money you must be dull enough to want it."
—G. K. Chesterton

"So far as I can remember, there is not one word in the Gospels in praise of intelligence."
—Bertrand Russell

Money and wisdom are useless unless applied thoughtfully to the world.

Do something with your observations.

"So far as I can remember, there is not one word in the Gospels in praise of intelligence."
—Bertrand Russell

"Be the first to say something obvious and achieve immortality."
—Marie von Ebner Eschenbach

State what you notice: you might be the first.

June 10

If you think of a solution, the problem
is half solved.

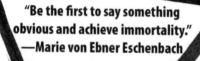
"Be the first to say something
obvious and achieve immortality."
—Marie von Ebner Eschenbach

"It is the greatest happiness
of the greatest number
that is the measure of
right and wrong."
—Jeremy Bentham

If common sense is
understood but
not applied,
people suffer.

It's never wrong to be helpful.

"It is the greatest happiness
of the greatest number that is the
measure of right and wrong."
—Jeremy Bentham

"It is better to be vaguely
right than precisely wrong."
—H. Wildon Carr

Aim your efforts toward a truth
and they'll be worthwhile.

Ambiguity is where opportunity lurks.

"It is better to be vaguely
right than precisely wrong."
—H. Wildon Carr

Don't be afraid of the weird, gray areas:
there is potential there.

"Now, my own suspicion is that
the universe is not only queerer
than we suppose but queerer
than we can suppose."
—J. B. S. Haldane

Think about anything for long, and it starts to feel beautifully absurd.

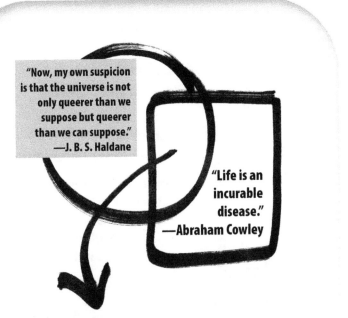

"Now, my own suspicion is that the universe is not only queerer than we suppose but queerer than we can suppose."
—J. B. S. Haldane

"Life is an incurable disease."
—Abraham Cowley

It's wild any of us are alive in the first place.

Science keeps increasing our potentials.

"Life is an incurable disease."
—Abraham Cowley

"One can measure the importance
of scientific work by the number
of earlier publications rendered
superfluous by it."
—David Hilbert

+

Our modern world is a massive
pile of miraculous discoveries.

June 15

**People everywhere are doing
amazing things.**

"One can measure the
importance of scientific work
by the number of earlier
publications rendered
superfluous by it."
—David Hilbert

"Life is a banquet,
and most poor
sons-of-bitches
are starving
to death! Live!"
—Jerome Lawrence

It's easy to
gorge on the
ever-growing
brilliance of
our species.

Be an exuberant example.

"Life is a banquet, and most poor sons-of-bitches are starving to death! Live!"
—Jerome Lawrence

Enthusiasm for life is contagious.

"Character is a diamond that scratches every other stone."
—Cyrus R. Bartol

True character can't hide from truth.

"Character is a diamond that scratches every other stone."
—Cyrus R. Bartol

"The historian's first duties are sacrilege and the mocking of false gods. They are his indispensible instruments for establishing the truth."
—Jules Michelet

There's no hiding from who you truly are. Embrace it honestly.

Truth doesn't wear a filter.

"The historian's first duties are sacrilege and the mocking of false gods. They are his indispensible instruments for establishing the truth."
—Jules Michelet

When it comes to information, absorbing and reflecting are the same action.

"Our growth depends not on how many experiences we devour, but on how many we digest."
—Ralph W. Sockman

**If we think deeply on any event,
we will feel a bit responsible.**

"Our growth depends not
on how many experiences
we devour, but on how
many we digest."
—Ralph W. Sockman

"The search for
someone to blame is
always successful."
—Robert Half

Taking responsibility is empowering.

June 20

Assigning blame is a coward's task.

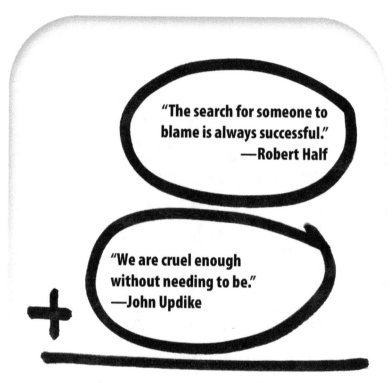

"The search for someone to blame is always successful."
—Robert Half

"We are cruel enough without needing to be."
—John Updike

The strongest people shoulder more than their share of blame.

Humans are frightening.

"We are cruel enough without needing to be."
—John Updike

Cruelty is never laudable.

"Wild animals never kill for sport. Man is the only one to whom torture and death of his fellow-creatures is amusing in itself."
—James A. Froude

The most dangerous predator on earth wears pants.

"Wild animals never kill for sport. Man is the only one to whom torture and death of his fellow-creatures is amusing in itself."
—James A. Froude

It's against our nature but in our interest to be nonviolent.

"Facts do not cease to exist because they are ignored."
—Aldous Huxley

We should remind ourselves that
life is short and miraculous.

"Facts do not cease to exist
because they are ignored."
—Aldous Huxley

Don't let common drudgeries overshadow
how fortunate we are to be alive.

"Our existence is but a brief
crack of light between two
eternities of darkness."
—Vladimir Nabokov

Speak the kindest words you can.

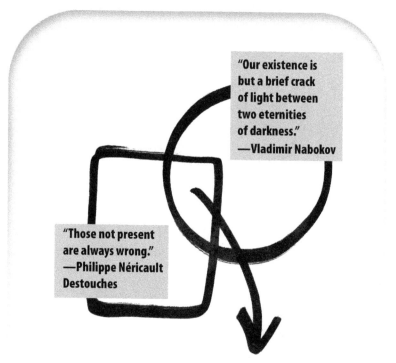

"Our existence is but a brief crack of light between two eternities of darkness."
—Vladimir Nabokov

"Those not present are always wrong."
—Philippe Néricault Destouches

Life is too short to gossip behind anyone's back.

**Petty gossip is an attempt
to dominate others.**

"Those not present are always wrong."
—Philippe Néricault Destouches

Be upfront with your feelings.

"Uniform pleasantness is rather a
defect than a faculty. It shows that a
man hasn't sense enough to know
whom to despise."
—Thomas Hardy

If you have to be brutally honest, be quick about it.

"Uniform pleasantness is rather a defect than a faculty. It shows that a man hasn't sense enough to know whom to despise."
—Thomas Hardy

Tell your truth politely.

"The most exhausting thing in life, I have discovered, is being insincere."
—Anne Morrow Lindbergh

Always be prepared to explain your actions.

"The most exhausting thing in life, I have discovered, is being insincere."
—Anne Morrow Lindbergh

"It's always easier to apologize for something you've already done than get approval for it in advance."
—Grace Murray Hopper

Doing what needs to be done often ruffles feathers.

Imagination can bend reality and rules.

"It's always easier to apologize for something you've already done than get approval for it in advance."
—Grace Murray Hopper

Seeing things that others don't means you'll be compelled to do what others won't.

"Haven't you sometimes seen a cloud that looked like a centaur? Or a leopard perhaps? Or a wolf? Or a bull?"
—Aristophanes

A playful mind stays sharp.

"Haven't you sometimes seen a cloud that looked like a centaur? Or a leopard perhaps? Or a wolf? Or a bull?"
—Aristophanes

Imagination obliterates boredom.

"No one grows old by living—only by losing interest in living."
—Marie Beynon Ray

No creative investigation is ever fruitless.

"No one grows old by living—only by losing interest in living."
—Marie Beynon Ray

"All things are filled full of signs, and it is the wise man who can learn about one thing from another."
—Plotinus

Curiosity is an anti-aging treatment.

It's healthy and human to be
overcome with emotion.

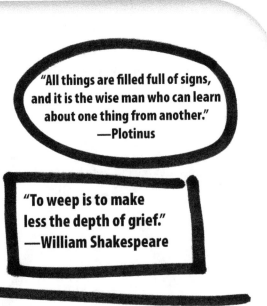

"All things are filled full of signs,
and it is the wise man who can learn
about one thing from another."
—Plotinus

"To weep is to make
less the depth of grief."
—William Shakespeare

Swallowing your feelings is
a form of cannibalism.

Fill the holes in your heart with new loves.

"To weep is to make less
the depth of grief."
—William Shakespeare

You can honor the lost with love for the newly found.

"If a tree dies, plant
another in its place."
—Linneaus

Love is a great motivation.

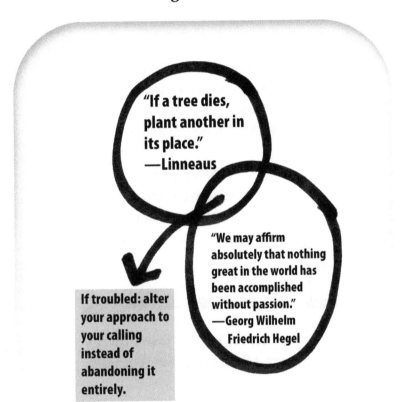

"If a tree dies, plant another in its place."
—Linneaus

If troubled: alter your approach to your calling instead of abandoning it entirely.

"We may affirm absolutely that nothing great in the world has been accomplished without passion."
—Georg Wilhelm Friedrich Hegel

July 4

You have only one lifetime to craft a legacy.

"We may affirm absolutely that nothing great in the world has been accomplished without passion."
—Georg Wilhelm Friedrich Hegel

"When we are planning for posterity, we ought to remember that virtue is not hereditary."
—Thomas Paine

Do the best you can and then trust the next generation to continue your work.

We are just small links in the chain of history.

"When we are planning for posterity, we ought to remember that virtue is not hereditary."
—Thomas Paine

You don't have to be a parent to trust the next generation.

"Insanity is hereditary. You get it from your children."
—Lillian Holstein

Nobody's perfect but everyone's lovable.

"Insanity is hereditary. You
get it from your children."
—Lillian Holstein

Unconditional love is egoless.

"Love is what's left of a
relationship after all the
selfishness has been removed."
—Cullen Hightower

A family without forgiveness is a hostage situation.

"Love is what's left of a relationship after all the selfishness has been removed."
—Cullen Hightower

Distrust your sense of righteousness.

"It is better that ten guilty persons escape than one innocent suffer."
—Sir William Blackstone

It's lonely up on the moral high-ground.

"It is better that ten guilty
persons escape than one
innocent suffer."
—Sir William Blackstone

No citizen can be of value to the community while in exile.

"The love of liberty is the love
of others; the love of power is
the love of ourselves."
—William Hazlitt

Be wary of your potential to be a selfish jerk.

"The love of liberty is the love of others;
the love of power is the love of ourselves."
—William Hazlitt

**Our worst tendencies can be
counter-balanced with generosity.**

"Evil is unspectacular and always human.
And shares our bed and eats at our table."
—W. H. Auden

July 10

**You have the most freedom
between your ears.**

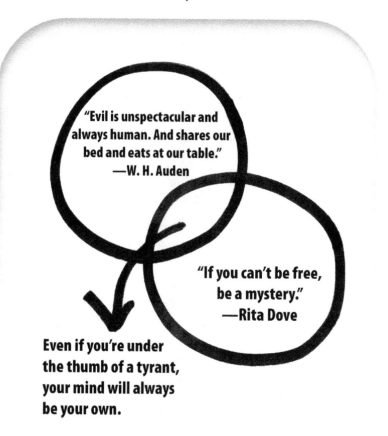

"Evil is unspectacular and
always human. And shares our
bed and eats at our table."
—W. H. Auden

"If you can't be free,
be a mystery."
—Rita Dove

Even if you're under
the thumb of a tyrant,
your mind will always
be your own.

Lofty ideas are tickets to freedom.

"If you can't be free,
be a mystery."
—Rita Dove

If you can imagine a better way of living, try to make it real.

"Free election of masters
does not abolish the
masters or the slaves."
—William L. Marcy

Question the systems in place.

"Free election of masters
does not abolish the
masters or the slaves."
—William L. Marcy

"When there is official
censorship it is a sign that
speech is serious. Where
there is none, it is pretty
certain that the official
spokesmen have all the
loud-speakers."
—Paul Goodman

The rules were
written to keep
certain people
in power.

Advertising lies to you about your needs.

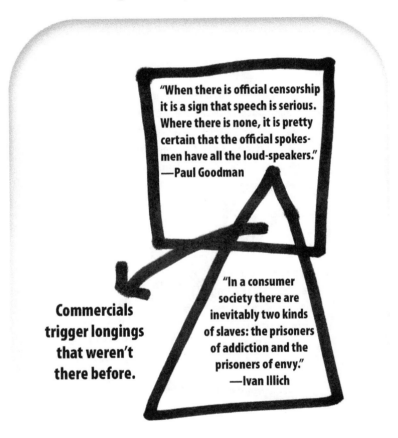

"When there is official censorship it is a sign that speech is serious. Where there is none, it is pretty certain that the official spokes-men have all the loud-speakers."
—Paul Goodman

Commercials trigger longings that weren't there before.

"In a consumer society there are inevitably two kinds of slaves: the prisoners of addiction and the prisoners of envy."
—Ivan Illich

July 14

Weakness by itself is no crime.

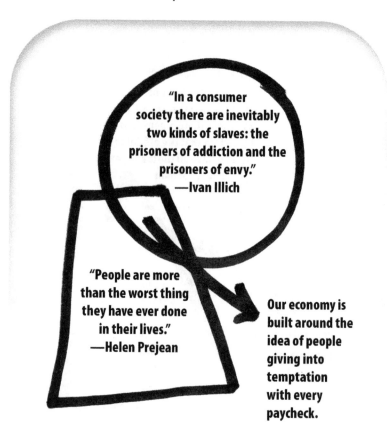

"In a consumer society there are inevitably two kinds of slaves: the prisoners of addiction and the prisoners of envy."
—Ivan Illich

"People are more than the worst thing they have ever done in their lives."
—Helen Prejean

Our economy is built around the idea of people giving into temptation with every paycheck.

Question the rules we subject one another to.

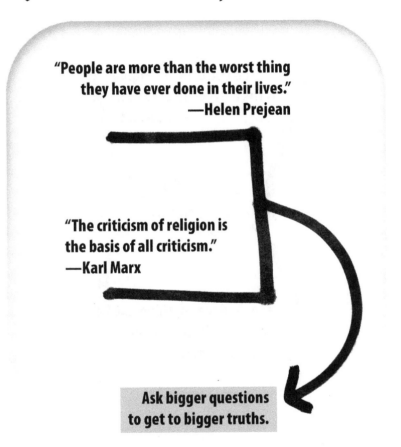

"People are more than the worst thing
they have ever done in their lives."
—Helen Prejean

"The criticism of religion is
the basis of all criticism."
—Karl Marx

Ask bigger questions
to get to bigger truths.

Get your information for legitimate sources.

"The criticism of religion
is the basis of all criticism."
—Karl Marx

Everybody has a perspective to spin.

"Never believe anything until
it has been officially denied."
—Claud Cockburn

Don't argue with ideologues.

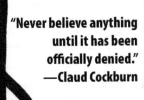

"Never believe anything until it has been officially denied."
—Claud Cockburn

"When dealing with people, remember you are not dealing with creatures of logic, but with creatures of emotion, creatures bristling with prejudice and motivated by pride and vanity."
—Dale Carnegie

People make decisions with their emotion, not with the facts.

All prejudices are manufactured.

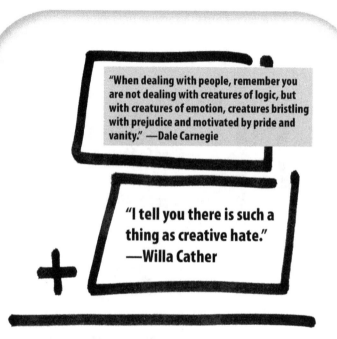

"When dealing with people, remember you are not dealing with creatures of logic, but with creatures of emotion, creatures bristling with prejudice and motivated by pride and vanity." —Dale Carnegie

"I tell you there is such a thing as creative hate." —Willa Cather

Legitimate goodness doesn't need corporate sponsorship.

Between the sound-bites, there is sentiment.

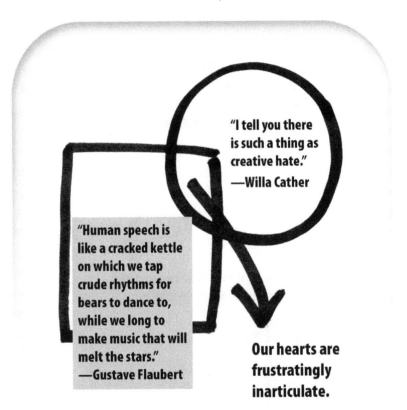

"I tell you there is such a thing as creative hate."
—Willa Cather

"Human speech is like a cracked kettle on which we tap crude rhythms for bears to dance to, while we long to make music that will melt the stars."
—Gustave Flaubert

Our hearts are frustratingly inarticulate.

Poetry says what common speech cannot.

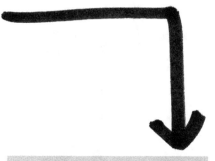

"Human speech is like a cracked kettle on which we tap crude rhythms for bears to dance to, while we long to make music that will melt the stars." —Gustave Flaubert

Not all sentiments can be expressed in day-to-day conversation.

"When the going gets weird, the weird turn pro." —Hunter S. Thompson

Freedom leads to nonconformity.

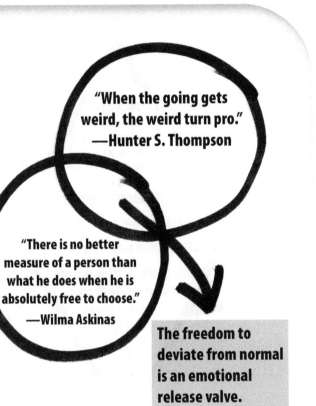

"When the going gets weird, the weird turn pro."
—Hunter S. Thompson

"There is no better measure of a person than what he does when he is absolutely free to choose."
—Wilma Askinas

The freedom to deviate from normal is an emotional release valve.

Take your vacation days.

"There is no better measure of a person than what he does when he is absolutely free to choose."
—Wilma Askinas

It's hard to know what we need.

"Do not mistake pleasure for happiness. They are a different breed of dogs."
—Josh Billings

Loneliness corrodes wellbeing.

"Do not mistake pleasure for happiness. They are a different breed of dogs."
—Josh Billings

"People are lonely because they build walls instead of bridges."
—Joseph Fort Newton

You'll never regret making time for your friends.

Fear makes us small.

"People are lonely
because they build walls
instead of bridges."
—Joseph Fort Newton

Communities thrive when doors are opened.

"We live, not as we wish
to, but as we can."
—Menander

Settling for 'good enough' prevents masterworks.

"We live, not as we wish to, but as we can."
—Menander

Being anything more than ordinary takes incredible resolve.

"Genius does what it must. Talent does what it can."
—Owen Meredith

Stand-out work all blends together eventually.

We all benefit from the music that was
written before we sat down to compose.

What's sexy won't be for long.

"We know that the nature of genius is to provide idiots with ideas twenty years later."
—Louis Aragon

Our perceptions shift with time.

"To me, old age is always fifteen years older than I am."
—Bernard M. Baruch

Kids these days need back-up.

"To me, old age is always
fifteen years older than I am."
—Bernard M. Baruch

Support the next
generation and they'll
do the same for you.

"What its children become, that
will the community become."
—Suzanne LaFollette

Education is the foundation of a society.

"What its children become, that will the community become."
—Suzanne LaFollette

"The best way to predict the future is to invent it."
—Allen Kay

Give young people the tools you wish you had.

Naysayers don't make history.

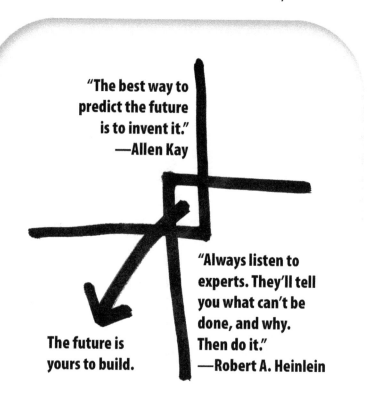

"The best way to predict the future is to invent it."
—Allen Kay

The future is yours to build.

"Always listen to experts. They'll tell you what can't be done, and why. Then do it."
—Robert A. Heinlein

You have to believe in yourself before anyone else will.

"Always listen to experts. They'll tell you what can't be done, and why. Then do it."
—Robert A. Heinlein

"Never doubt that a small group of committed people can change the world: Indeed, it is the only thing that ever has."
—Margaret Mead

Determination prompts change.

You are the best expert on your own work.

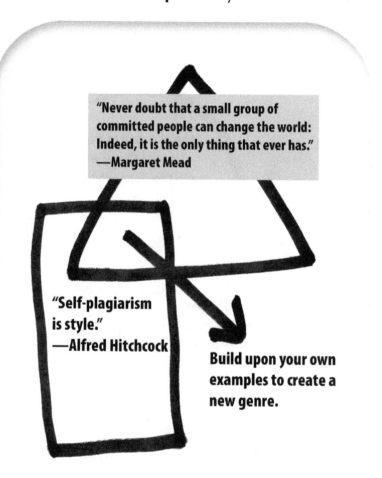

"Never doubt that a small group of committed people can change the world: Indeed, it is the only thing that ever has."
—Margaret Mead

"Self-plagiarism is style."
—Alfred Hitchcock

Build upon your own examples to create a new genre.

**Honest self-evaluation leads
to self-improvement.**

"Self-plagiarism is style."
—Alfred Hitchcock

Even great work can be improved upon.

"Humility is to make a
right estimate of oneself."
—Charles H. Spurgeon

Educated citizens result in a free society.

"Humility is to make a right estimate of oneself."
—Charles H. Spurgeon

Spread thoughtfulness to enjoy liberty.

"Education makes people easy to lead but difficult to drive; easy to govern, but impossible to enslave."
—Omar N. Bradley

A life of the mind improves life in general.

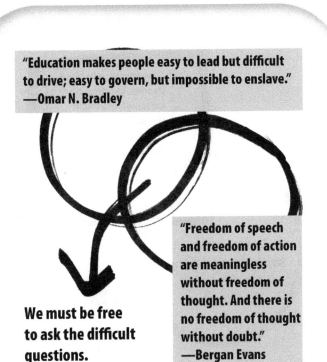

"Education makes people easy to lead but difficult to drive; easy to govern, but impossible to enslave."
—Omar N. Bradley

We must be free to ask the difficult questions.

"Freedom of speech and freedom of action are meaningless without freedom of thought. And there is no freedom of thought without doubt."
—Bergan Evans

Leaders must earn their roles.

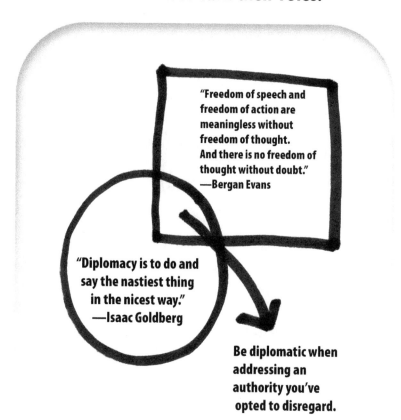

"Freedom of speech and
freedom of action are
meaningless without
freedom of thought.
And there is no freedom of
thought without doubt."
—Bergan Evans

"Diplomacy is to do and
say the nastiest thing
in the nicest way."
—Isaac Goldberg

Be diplomatic when
addressing an
authority you've
 opted to disregard.

We're here because we've all
decided we matter.

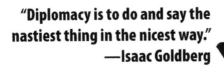

"Diplomacy is to do and say the
nastiest thing in the nicest way."
—Isaac Goldberg

"There is but one truly serious philosophical
problem, and that is suicide. Judging whether life
is or is not worth living amounts to answering the
fundamental question of philosophy."
—Albert Camus

The worst thing
anyone can ever
hear is that they
don't matter.

Never listen to a voice that belittles you.

"There is but one truly serious philosophical problem, and that is suicide. Judging whether life is or is not worth living amounts to answering the fundamental question of philosophy."
—Albert Camus

It's the voice in your head that always shouts the loudest.

"The most potent weapon in the hands of the oppressor is the mind of the oppressed."
—Steve Biko

Never let your boss's voice into your private thoughts.

"The most potent weapon in the hands of the oppressor is the mind of the oppressed."
—Steve Biko

"There is only one way to success—to be able to spend your life in your own way."
—Christopher Morley

True wealth is the freedom to nap whenever you want.

Bathrooms have doors for reasons.

"There is only one way to success—to be able to spend your life in your own way."
—Christopher Morley

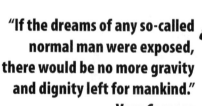

Most of our nastiest secrets are too mundane to tell.

"If the dreams of any so-called normal man were exposed, there would be no more gravity and dignity left for mankind."
—Vera Caspary

We all crave silly stuff.

"If the dreams of any so-called normal man were exposed, there would be no more gravity and dignity left for mankind."
—Vera Caspary

"There is only one good: knowledge, and one evil: ignorance."
—Socrates

Knowing that, deep down, we're all kind of vain and greedy is somehow freeing.

We ignore death as long as we can.

"There is only one good: knowledge,
and one evil: ignorance."
—Socrates

"Death borders
upon our birth,
and our cradle
stands in the grave."
—Joseph Hall

Acceptance of our
mortality drives
us to make the
most of our lives.

Live as much and as intensely as you can.

"Death borders upon our birth, and our cradle stands in the grave."
—Joseph Hall

"It is better to wear out than rust out."
—Richard Cumberland

Life's too short to be on the sofa so often.

Do what you can with the body you have.

"It is better to wear
out than rust out."
—Richard Cumberland

Change who you see in the mirror and
you'll change your entire life.

"It is no use to blame
the looking glass if your
face is awry."
—Nikolai Vasilievich Gogol

Good people see no ugly faces.

"It is no use to blame
the looking glass if
your face is awry."
—Nikolai Vasilievich Gogol

Everyone is stunning in their own ways.

"The perception of
beauty is a moral test."
—Henry David Thoreau

A carefully structured compliment is a kindness.

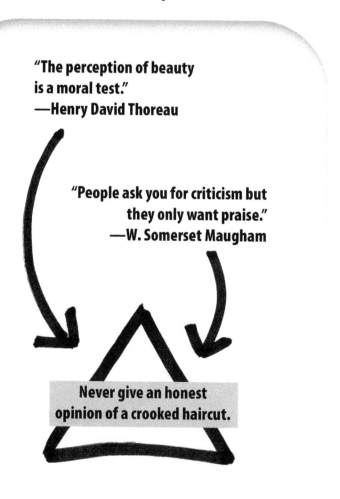

"The perception of beauty is a moral test."
—Henry David Thoreau

"People ask you for criticism but they only want praise."
—W. Somerset Maugham

Never give an honest opinion of a crooked haircut.

To be well spoken, be well read.

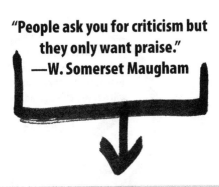

"People ask you for criticism but they only want praise."
—W. Somerset Maugham

You'll always know what to say if you've read enough.

"Libraries will get you through a time with no money better than money will get you through a time with no libraries."
—Ann Herbert

A good book is a loyal friend.

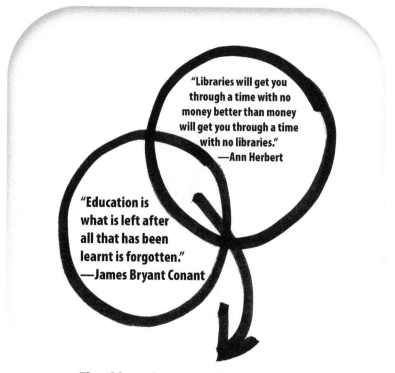

"Libraries will get you through a time with no money better than money will get you through a time with no libraries."
—Ann Herbert

"Education is what is left after all that has been learnt is forgotten."
—James Bryant Conant

The things that stick with you are the things that you react to emotionally.

What we know and what we act on are unfortunately not always the same.

"Education is what is left after all that has been learnt is forgotten."
—James Bryant Conant

We learn from our mistakes, but not nearly enough.

"History is indeed little more than the register of the crimes, follies, and misfortunes of mankind."
—Edward Gibbon

Documenting history is an artistic practice.

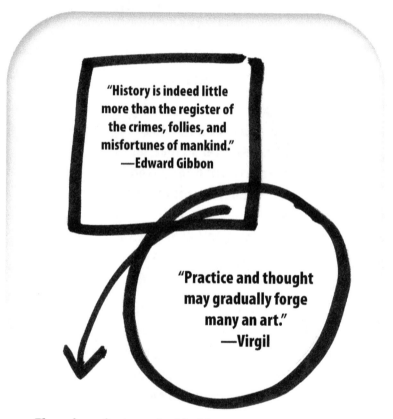

"History is indeed little more than the register of the crimes, follies, and misfortunes of mankind."
—Edward Gibbon

"Practice and thought may gradually forge many an art."
—Virgil

There is majesty embedded in every event.

The art of persuasion is a subtle art indeed.

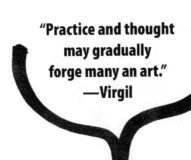

"Practice and thought
may gradually
forge many an art."
—Virgil

Telling the truth in a way people will
accept is a very valuable skill.

"Truth often suffers more
from the heat of its defenders
than from the arguments
of its opposers."
—William Penn

Military propaganda is never gory.

"Truth often suffers more from the heat of its defenders than from the arguments of its opposers."
—William Penn

A euphemism that makes horror palatable is an outright lie.

"A war, even the most victorious, is a national misfortune."
—Helmuth von Moltke

When terrible things happen, we cannot afford not to study them.

"A war, even the most victorious, is a national misfortune."
—Helmuth von Moltke

"The historian is a prophet in reverse."
—Friedrich von Schlegel

The main question to ask of history is, "Why?"

There are precious clues hiding everywhere.

"The historian is a prophet in reverse."
—Friedrich von Schlegel

Always be ready to notice something important.

"In the fields of observation chance
favors only the prepared mind."
—Louis Pasteur

Pompous characters are unintentionally hilarious.

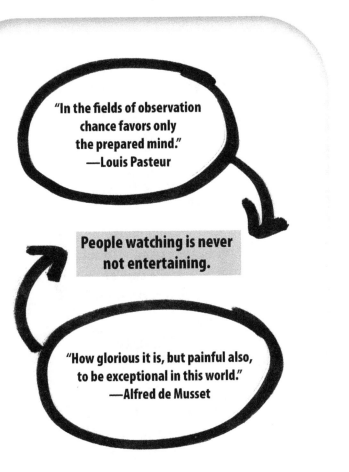

"In the fields of observation chance favors only the prepared mind."
—Louis Pasteur

People watching is never not entertaining.

"How glorious it is, but painful also, to be exceptional in this world."
—Alfred de Musset

If you take yourself too seriously,
nobody else will.

"How glorious it is, but painful also,
to be exceptional in this world."
—Alfred de Musset

Your most
exaggerated attribute
is the core of
your caricature.

"Humor is emotional chaos
remembered in tranquility."
—James Thurber

Temper laughter with somberness and vice versa so as to not go insane.

"Humor is emotional chaos remembered in tranquility."
—James Thurber

Too much of anything is boring and poisonous.

"Every form of addiction is bad, no matter whether the narcotic be alcohol or morphine or idealism."
—Carl Gustav Jung

Highbrow and lowbrow are subjective classifications.

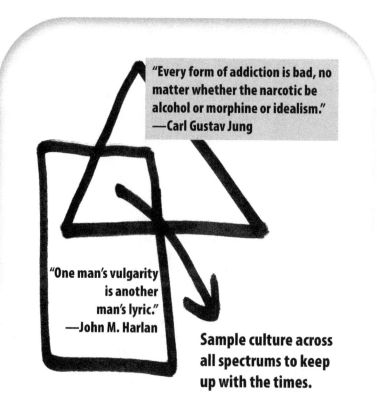

"Every form of addiction is bad, no matter whether the narcotic be alcohol or morphine or idealism."
—Carl Gustav Jung

"One man's vulgarity is another man's lyric."
—John M. Harlan

Sample culture across all spectrums to keep up with the times.

When we express ourselves, we broadcast who we are.

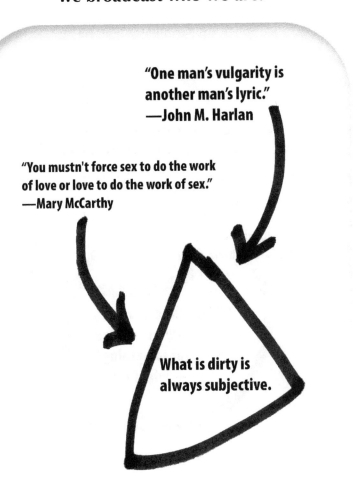

"One man's vulgarity is another man's lyric."
—John M. Harlan

"You mustn't force sex to do the work of love or love to do the work of sex."
—Mary McCarthy

What is dirty is always subjective.

The absolute value of anything is never measured in dollars.

"You mustn't force sex to do the work of love or love to do the work of sex."
—Mary McCarthy

By endlessly evaluating things, we take the charm out of them.

"They say everything in the world is good for something."
—John Dryden

There's always an upside.

"They say everything in the
world is good for something."
—John Dryden

If you study anything hard enough, you'll find
something to like about it.

"My favorite
thing about the internet
is that you get to go
into the private world of real
creeps without having to smell them."
—Penn Jilette

Anonymity is no excuse for abuse.

"My favorite thing about the internet is that you get to go into the private world of real creeps without having to smell them."
—Penn Jilette

"Epithets are not arguments. Abuse does not persuade."
—Robert Green Ingersoll

It's amazing what people will say when they don't believe it will get traced back to them.

Scolding doesn't change anyone's fate.

"Epithets are not arguments. Abuse does not persuade."
—Robert Green Ingersoll

Encouragement is more useful than browbeating.

"Destiny: a tyrant's authority for crime and a fool's excuse for failure."
—Ambrose Bierce

Identities change all the time.

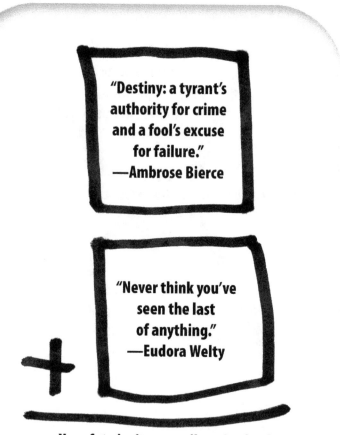

"Destiny: a tyrant's authority for crime and a fool's excuse for failure."
—Ambrose Bierce

"Never think you've seen the last of anything."
—Eudora Welty

Your fate isn't set until you're dead.

You'll be amazed at what manages to grow back.

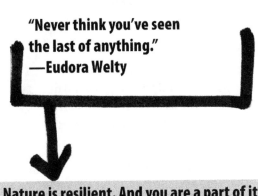

"Never think you've seen the last of anything."
—Eudora Welty

Nature is resilient. And you are a part of it.

"Those who contemplate the beauty of the earth will find reserves of strength that will endure as long as life lasts."
—Rachel Carson

Knowing what is truly valuable is vital.

"Those who contemplate
the beauty of the earth will find
reserves of strength that
will endure as long as life lasts."
—Rachel Carson

There are possible futures for our world that are
not currently offered, but must be built.

"If they can get you asking
the wrong questions,
they don't have to worry
about the answers."
—Thomas Pynchon

If you think you have no good options,
you haven't looked hard enough.

"If they can get you asking the wrong questions,
they don't have to worry about the answers."
—Thomas Pynchon

"There is no trap so deadly
as the trap you set for yourself."
—Raymond Chandler

Don't constrain yourself to the obvious choices.

A rut is a manifestation of passivity.

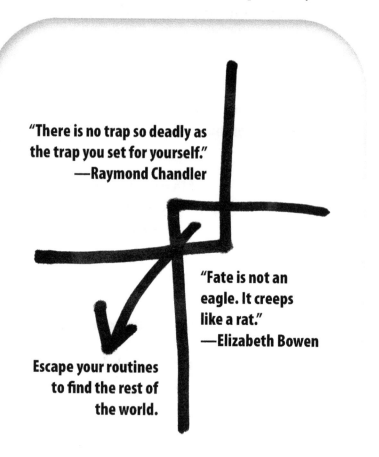

"There is no trap so deadly as the trap you set for yourself."
—Raymond Chandler

"Fate is not an eagle. It creeps like a rat."
—Elizabeth Bowen

Escape your routines to find the rest of the world.

Half the value in any idea is the marketing of it.

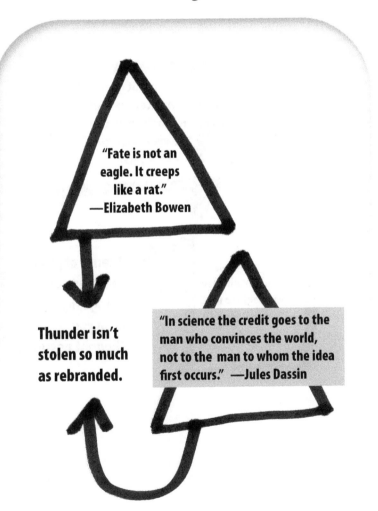

"Fate is not an eagle. It creeps like a rat."
—Elizabeth Bowen

Thunder isn't stolen so much as rebranded.

"In science the credit goes to the man who convinces the world, not to the man to whom the idea first occurs." —Jules Dassin

**Decide what you want to be
known for and do it.**

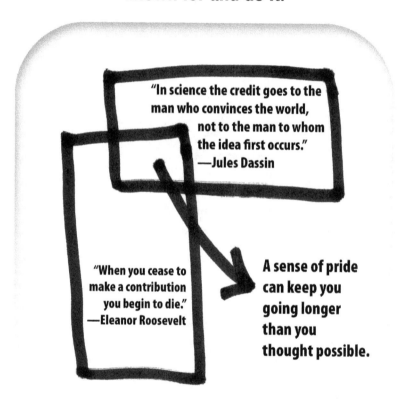

"In science the credit goes to the
man who convinces the world,
not to the man to whom
the idea first occurs."
—Jules Dassin

"When you cease to
make a contribution
you begin to die."
—Eleanor Roosevelt

A sense of pride
can keep you
going longer
than you
thought possible.

Keep up or be left behind.

"When you cease to make a contribution you begin to die."
—Eleanor Roosevelt

"Whoever said, 'if it ain't broke don't fix it,' probably never heard of preventative maintenance."
—Steven Kasper

Tune-up your resolve to stay on your chosen track.

Avoid breakdowns. Take care of yourself.

"Whoever said, 'if it ain't broke don't fix it,' probably
never heard of preventative maintenance."
—Steven Kasper

**A functional person needs a
reason to keep going.**

"Resistance is the secret of joy!"
—Alice Walker

Consistency of effort makes it successful.

"Resistance is the secret of joy!"
—Alice Walker

Push against what would destroy you.

"Discipline without freedom
is tyranny. Freedom without
discipline is chaos."
—Cullen Hightower

Age needn't slow your mind.

"Discipline without freedom is tyranny. Freedom without discipline is chaos."
—Cullen Hightower

"You can judge your age by the amount of pains you feel when you come in contact with a new idea."
—John Nuveen

Learning new things can make you feel younger than you look.

Absurdity is a form of humor.

"You can judge your age by the
amount of pains you feel when
you come in contact
with a new idea."
—John Nuveen

Let yourself be intrigued by strange new things.

"The magnificent
and the ridiculous are
so close that they touch."
—Bertrand de Fontenelle

September 14

The ability to spot ironies helps keep us honest.

"The magnificent and the ridiculous are so close that they touch."
—Bertrand de Fontenelle

"The defect of equality is that we only desire it with our superiors."
—Henry Becque

Laugh at hypocrisy and it will wither.

May the best people become
your dearest friends.

"The defect of equality
is that we only desire it
with our superiors."
—Henry Becque

There's no place for hierarchy in friendship.

"Fate chooses
our relatives, we
choose our friends."
—Jacques Delille

Home is where your people are.

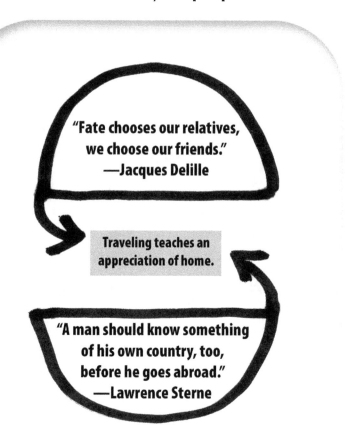

"Fate chooses our relatives,
we choose our friends."
—Jacques Delille

Traveling teaches an
appreciation of home.

"A man should know something
of his own country, too,
before he goes abroad."
—Lawrence Sterne

**You will meet brilliant people
anywhere you go.**

"A man should know something
of his own country, too, before
he goes abroad."
—Lawrence Sterne

"Genius is of no country."
—Charles Churchill

The more
places you go,
the fewer people
you fear.

September 18

Whoever claims to be a genius
probably isn't.

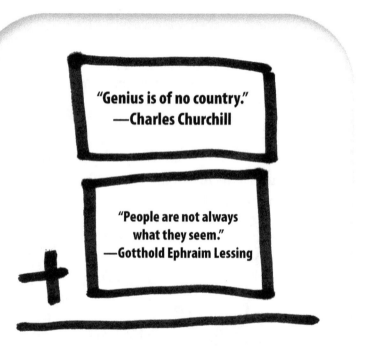

"Genius is of no country."
—Charles Churchill

"People are not always
what they seem."
—Gotthold Ephraim Lessing

Those who don't brag often have
plenty to brag about. And vice versa.

The only person it's impossible to lie
to is yourself.

"People are not always what they seem."
—Gotthold Ephraim Lessing

Everyone leads
a secret life
inside their
own head.

"Deceive not thy physician, confessor, nor lawyer."
—George Herbert

When in doubt, talk it out.

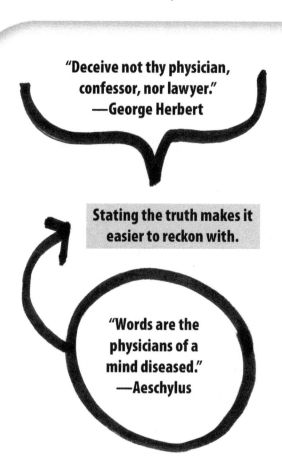

"Deceive not thy physician,
confessor, nor lawyer."
—George Herbert

Stating the truth makes it
easier to reckon with.

"Words are the
physicians of a
mind diseased."
—Aeschylus

Don't underestimate the healing power of words.

"Words are the physicians of a mind diseased."
—Aeschylus

Read something lyrical to set your mind at ease.

"Syllables govern the world."
—John Selden

The letters of the law can always
be reorganized.

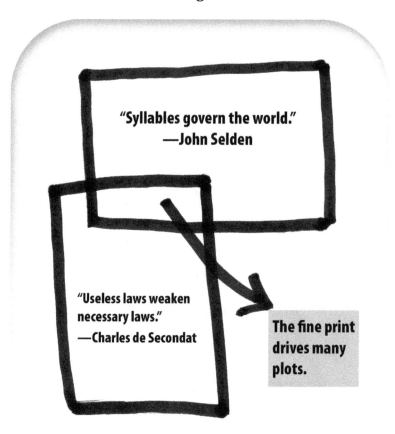

"Syllables govern the world."
—John Selden

"Useless laws weaken
necessary laws."
—Charles de Secondat

The fine print
drives many
plots.

Just because something's illegal doesn't mean it's wrong, and vice versa.

"Useless laws weaken necessary laws."
—Charles de Secondat

Work for justice, especially when the law is against it.

"Laws grind the poor, and rich men rule the law."
—Oliver Goldsmith

Endeavor to be contemplative,
not reactionary.

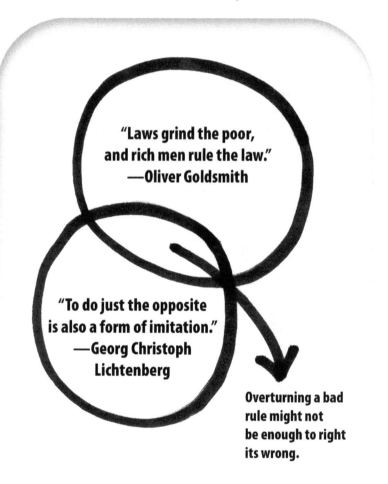

"Laws grind the poor,
and rich men rule the law."
—Oliver Goldsmith

"To do just the opposite
is also a form of imitation."
—Georg Christoph
Lichtenberg

Overturning a bad
rule might not
be enough to right
its wrong.

Oppose wrong views, but from your own angle.

"To do just the opposite is also a form of imitation."
—Georg Christoph Lichtenberg

Waging peace is a lifelong undertaking.

"There is never a good war or a bad peace."
—Benjamin Franklin

Some things are simply, genuinely good.
Try not to be wary of them.

"There is never a
good war or a bad peace."
—Benjamin Franklin

"A little credulity
helps one on through life
very smoothly."
—Elizabeth Cleghorn Gaskell

Believe in goodness unless
given a viable reason to doubt it.

Believe what is in front of you.

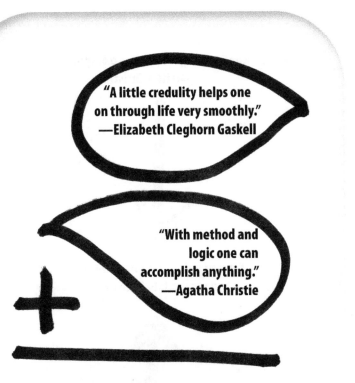

"A little credulity helps one on through life very smoothly."
—Elizabeth Cleghorn Gaskell

"With method and logic one can accomplish anything."
—Agatha Christie

Only cynics question the existence of absolutely everything.

Give yourself deadlines to get more done.

"With method and logic one can accomplish anything."
—Agatha Christie

You can putter your life away unless
you schedule time not to.

"Work expands to fill the time available for its completion."
—C. Northcote Parkinson

You can learn a lot while dong nothing.

"Work expands to fill
the time available for
its completion."
—C. Northcote Parkinson

A day can never be entirely misspent.

"Experience is the
name everyone gives to
their mistakes."
—Oscar Wilde

Wandering is a great way to figure
out where you want to go.

"Experience is the
name everyone gives
to their mistakes."
—Oscar Wilde

"If you don't know where you're
going, you will probably end
up somewhere else."
—Laurence J. Peter

There are interesting things
behind every wrong turn.

If you want to find yourself, you have
to take the journey alone.

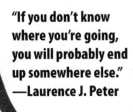

"If you don't know
where you're going,
you will probably end
up somewhere else."
—Laurence J. Peter

Other people influence our lives in ways
we often don't notice until it's too late.

"Don't accept rides
from strange men, and
remember that all men
are strange as hell."
—Robin Morgan

If you get a bad vibe from someone, move on.

"Don't accept rides from strange men, and remember that all men are strange as hell."
—Robin Morgan

Better safe than sorry when it comes to people who give you the creeps.

"Time wounds all heels."
—Frank Case

Hope that Karma is real, but don't plan on it.

"Time wounds all heels."
—Frank Case

"You can never plan
the future by the past."
—Edmund Burke

Forgive but maintain
your boundaries.

A hope is not a game plan.

"You can never plan the future by the past."
—Edmund Burke

If you want something to happen, do more than hope.

"Nothing is so firmly believed as what is least known."
—Michel Eyquem de Montaigne

Utopia has yet to be experienced.

"Nothing is so firmly believed
as what is least known."
—Michel Eyquem de Montaigne

Utopia is a goal, not a place.

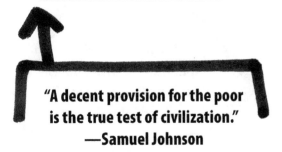

"A decent provision for the poor
is the true test of civilization."
—Samuel Johnson

Peace is never equally distributed.

"A decent provision for the poor is the true test of civilization."
—Samuel Johnson

A good government takes care of all its citizens.

"If peace cannot be maintained with honor, it is no longer peace."
—Lord John Russell

There's enough to go around, but our supply chains are tangled.

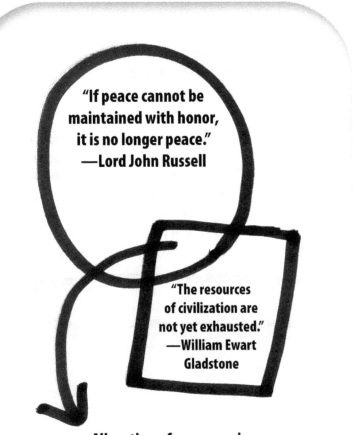

"If peace cannot be maintained with honor, it is no longer peace."
—Lord John Russell

"The resources of civilization are not yet exhausted."
—William Ewart Gladstone

Allocation of resources is always a political issue.

We are all intimately connected.

"The resources of civilization
are not yet exhausted."
—William Ewart Gladstone

"If we assume that the last breath of,
say, Julius Caesar has by now become
thoroughly scattered through
the atmosphere, then the chances are
that each of us inhales one molecule
of it with every breath we take."
—James Jeans

We all share this world without even meaning to.

An idea put into words can be shared a billion times.

"If we assume that the last breath of, say, Julius Caesar has by now become thoroughly scattered through the atmosphere, then the chances are that each of us inhales one molecule of it with every breath we take."
—James Jeans

Poetry can guide reality.

"Ideas are to literature what light is to painting."
—Paul Bourget

Words motivate.

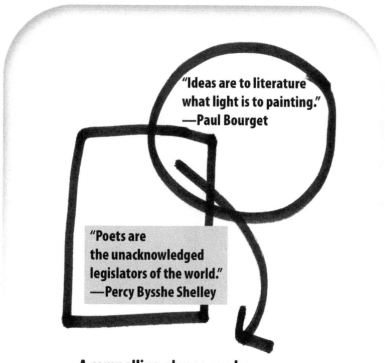

"Ideas are to literature what light is to painting."
—Paul Bourget

"Poets are the unacknowledged legislators of the world."
—Percy Bysshe Shelley

A compelling phrase can be
the fulcrum upon which
a revolution turns.

True and false are not the same as truth and lies.

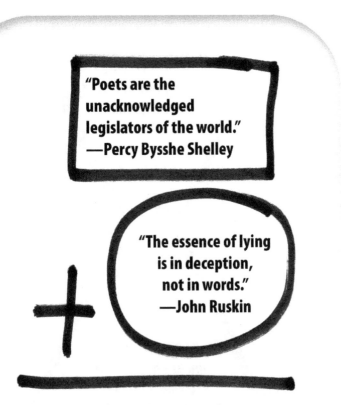

"Poets are the unacknowledged legislators of the world."
—Percy Bysshe Shelley

+

"The essence of lying is in deception, not in words."
—John Ruskin

Fiction writers don't lie.

The harder something is to rationalize,
the sooner it needs to stop.

"The essence of lying is in
deception, not in words."
—John Ruskin

Don't try to convince yourself that something bad is good.

"Ask yourself whether
you are happy, and
you cease to be so."
—John Stuart Mill

Enjoy the waves of joy that wash over you.

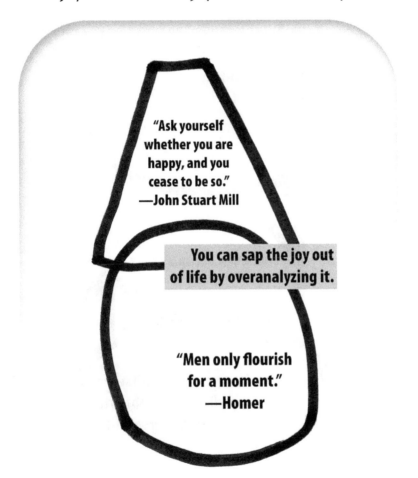

"Ask yourself whether you are happy, and you cease to be so."
—John Stuart Mill

You can sap the joy out of life by overanalyzing it.

"Men only flourish for a moment."
—Homer

Better to be a has-been than a never-was.

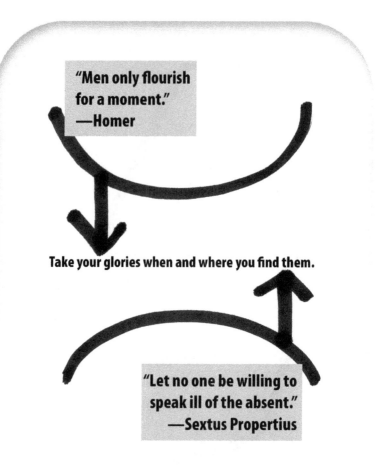

"Men only flourish for a moment."
—Homer

Take your glories when and where you find them.

"Let no one be willing to speak ill of the absent."
—Sextus Propertius

Speak as if you're being recorded.

"Let no one be willing to
speak ill of the absent."
—Sextus Propertius

You'll never regret saying kind words.

"Conscience is the inner
voice which warns us
somebody might be looking."
—H.L. Mencken

Making history isn't always a noble act.

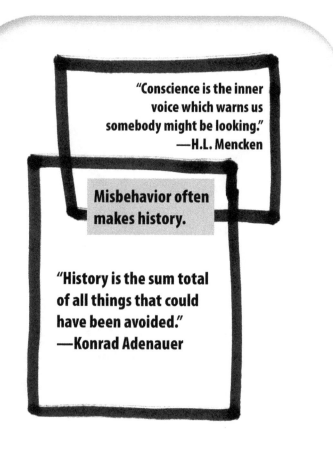

"Conscience is the inner voice which warns us somebody might be looking."
—H.L. Mencken

Misbehavior often makes history.

"History is the sum total of all things that could have been avoided."
—Konrad Adenauer

If you're not sure you should tell a joke, don't.

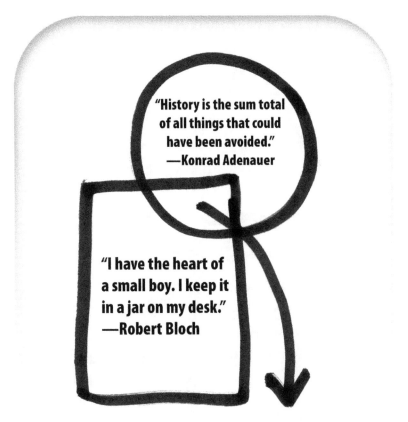

"History is the sum total of all things that could have been avoided."
—Konrad Adenauer

"I have the heart of a small boy. I keep it in a jar on my desk."
—Robert Bloch

The darker the humor, the more likely it will offend.

Team players accept each other's quirks.

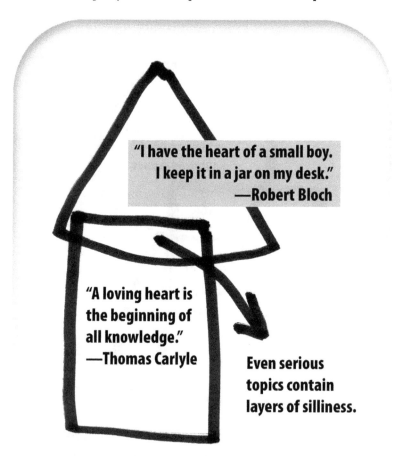

"I have the heart of a small boy.
I keep it in a jar on my desk."
—Robert Bloch

"A loving heart is
the beginning of
all knowledge."
—Thomas Carlyle

Even serious
topics contain
layers of silliness.

Be patient with insomniacs.

"A loving heart is the beginning of all knowledge."
—Thomas Carlyle

Nightly unconsciousness makes thoughtfulness possible.

"Sleep is death without the responsibility."
—Fran Lebowitz

Every night, we get a break from work
and worry when we sleep.

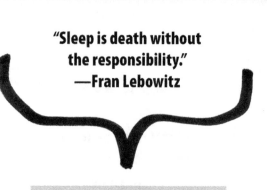

"Sleep is death without
the responsibility."
—Fran Lebowitz

Exhaustion happens to us all.

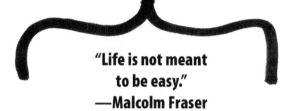

"Life is not meant
to be easy."
—Malcolm Fraser

Always leverage what you have already.

"Life is not meant to be easy."
—Malcolm Fraser

"Those who know how to win are more numerous than those who know how to make proper use of their victories."
—Polybius

Success is a win well leveraged.

Better to be clever than strong.

"Those who know how to win are more numerous than those who know how to make proper use of their victories."
—Polybius

"The monuments of wit survive the monuments of power."
—Francis Bacon

Strength is easily exploited by nimble minds.

Your legacy is your mind's work.

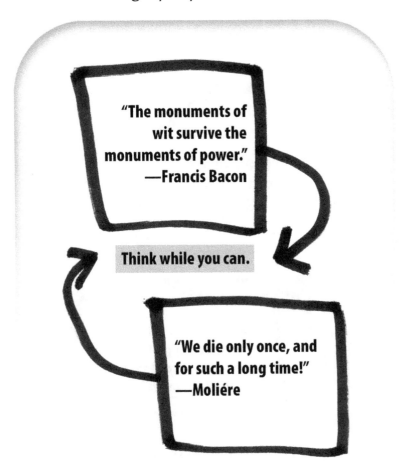

"The monuments of wit survive the monuments of power."
—Francis Bacon

Think while you can.

"We die only once, and for such a long time!"
—Moliére

You'll never really understand someone else's choices, but you can respect them anyway.

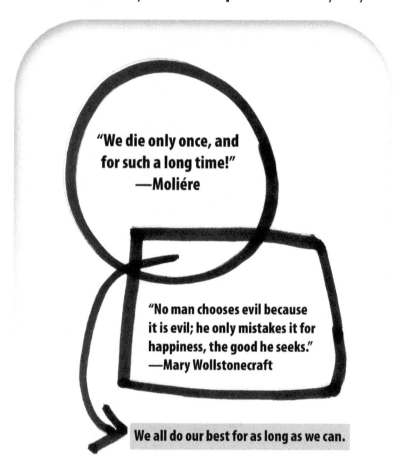

"We die only once, and for such a long time!"
—Moliére

"No man chooses evil because it is evil; he only mistakes it for happiness, the good he seeks."
—Mary Wollstonecraft

We all do our best for as long as we can.

We talk in extremes but rarely inhabit them.

"No man chooses evil
because it is evil; he
only mistakes it for
happiness, the good
he seeks."
—Mary Wollstonecraft

Most of our lives are lived in the gray areas.

"Pure and complete
sorrow is as impossible as
pure and complete joy."
—Leo Tolstoy

Lessening pain is a noble cause.

"Pure and complete sorrow is as impossible as pure and complete joy."
—Leo Tolstoy

Wealth is always relative.

"The greatest of our evils and the worst of our crimes is poverty."
—George Bernard Shaw

What is obvious to you is obviously false
to other people.

"The greatest of our
evils and the worst
of our crimes is poverty."
—George Bernard Shaw

Some people really think poverty is deserved.

"Convictions are more
dangerous enemies of
truth than lies."
—Friedrich Nietzsche

Beware the man who states
his opinions as facts.

"Convictions are more dangerous
enemies of truth than lies."
—Friedrich Nietzsche

You can't argue with a self-appointed expert.

"A bore is a man who, when you
ask him how he is, tells you."
—Bert L. Taylor

Small people try to take down great ones.

"A bore is a man who, when you ask him how he is, tells you."
—Bert L. Taylor

"When a true Genius appears in the World, you will know him by this Sign; that the Dunces are in Confederacy against him."
—Jonathan Swift

If a lot of bores rant against somebody: get on that somebody's side.

Be glad that you'll never know everything that's said about you.

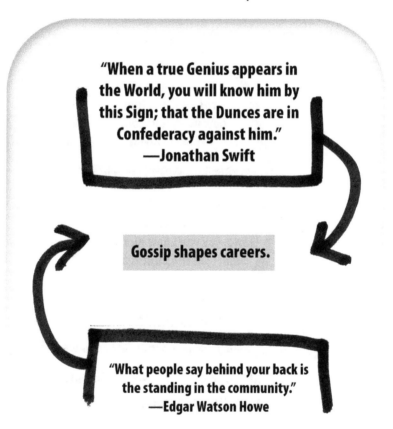

"When a true Genius appears in the World, you will know him by this Sign; that the Dunces are in Confederacy against him."
—Jonathan Swift

Gossip shapes careers.

"What people say behind your back is the standing in the community."
—Edgar Watson Howe

If you trust someone, ask what they've heard about you.

"What people say behind
your back is the standing
in the community."
—Edgar Watson Howe

Good friends defend each other.

"Put not your trust in money
but put your money in trust."
—Oliver Wendell Holmes

A good reputation is a precious thing.

"Put not your trust in money but put your money in trust."
—Oliver Wendell Holmes

"Character is higher than intellect."
—Ralph Waldo Emerson

Align with good people to avoid trouble.

If you want to be happy, be forthright.

"Character is higher
than intellect."
—Ralph Waldo Emerson

"Happiness, whether in
business or private life, leaves
very little trace in history."
—Fernand Braudel

Trustworthy people tend
to be happier, because
they have less drama
to deal with.

If it sounds like there's a catch, it's probably a bad deal.

"Happiness, whether in business or private life, leaves very little trace in history."
—Fernand Braudel

We recall resentments more easily than we can moments of joy.

"Favors cease to be favors when there are conditions attached to them."
—Thornton Wilder

Sneaky people keep good notes.

"Favors cease to be favors when there are conditions attached to them."
—Thornton Wilder

Good friends rarely keep score.

"A liar should have a good memory."
—Quintilian

Telling lies is an avoidable stress.

"A liar should have a good memory."
—Quintilian

"In silence man can most
readily preserve his dignity."
—Meister Eckhart

Silence prevents a lot of regret.

Give at least a little credit to anyone who dares to create.

"In silence man can most readily preserve his dignity."
—Meister Eckhart

Snotty commentary discourages valid efforts.

"Criticism is easy, art is difficult."
—Philippe Destouches

Critics are lonely because people fear
becoming their next target.

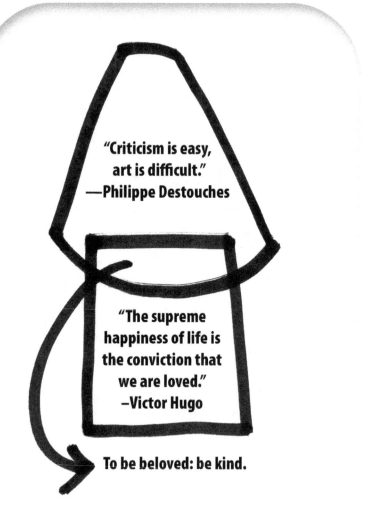

"Criticism is easy,
art is difficult."
—Philippe Destouches

"The supreme
happiness of life is
the conviction that
we are loved."
–Victor Hugo

To be beloved: be kind.

You are enough. Don't believe anyone
who says otherwise.

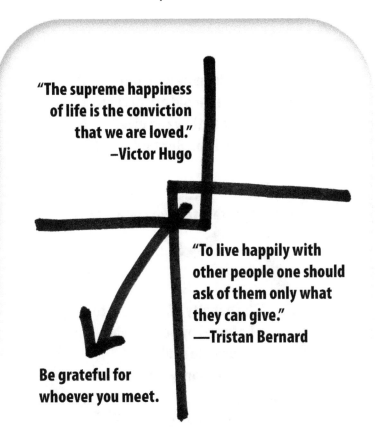

"The supreme happiness
of life is the conviction
that we are loved."
–Victor Hugo

"To live happily with
other people one should
ask of them only what
they can give."
—Tristan Bernard

Be grateful for
whoever you meet.

Use your success to lift up others,
not look down on them.

"To live happily with other
people one should ask of them
only what they can give."
—Tristan Bernard

Don't let success turn you into a snob.

"The penalty of success is to
be bored by people who
used to snub you."
—Nancy Astor

Treat everyone as your equal, especially
when you have power.

"The penalty of success is to be bored
by people who used to snub you."
—Nancy Astor

Respect, and the lack of it,
are both sharp sensations.

"What you do not want to do to
yourself, do not do to others."
—Confucius

Never assume some else is stupid.

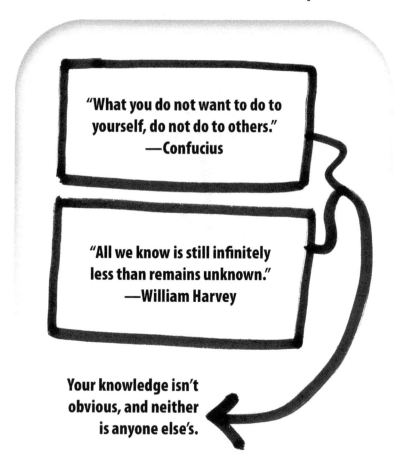

"What you do not want to do to yourself, do not do to others."
—Confucius

"All we know is still infinitely less than remains unknown."
—William Harvey

Your knowledge isn't obvious, and neither is anyone else's.

It's impossible not to learn something from even the worst book.

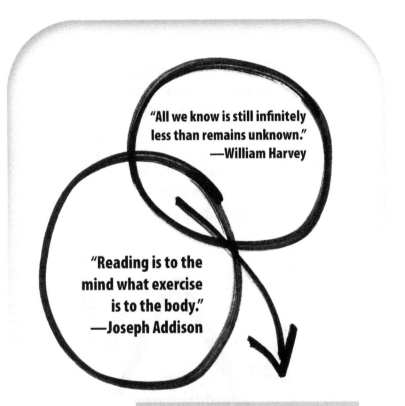

"All we know is still infinitely less than remains unknown."
—William Harvey

"Reading is to the mind what exercise is to the body."
—Joseph Addison

Every page of every book can be a revelation to an open mind.

Trashy books are enjoyable because they're harmless gossip.

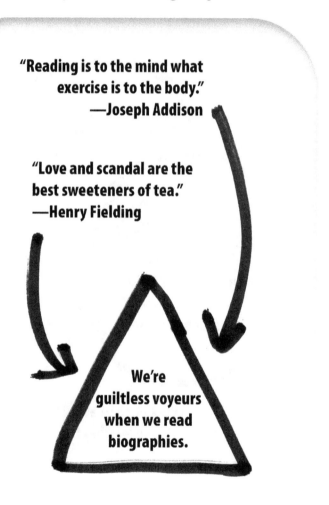

"Reading is to the mind what exercise is to the body."
—Joseph Addison

"Love and scandal are the best sweeteners of tea."
—Henry Fielding

We're guiltless voyeurs when we read biographies.

Gossip never sleeps.

"Love and scandal are the
best sweeteners of tea."
—Henry Fielding

Good neighbors close their drapes.

"Every man is surrounded by a
neighborhood of voluntary spies."
—Jane Austen

It's exhausting keeping up with everyone.

"Every man is surrounded by a
neighborhood of voluntary spies."
—Jane Austen

"The wages of sin are death, but
by the time taxes are taken out,
it's just sort of a tired feeling."
—Paula Poundstone

When everyone's poking in your business,
that business feels less profitable.

Paying a lot in taxes is a good
problem to have.

"The wages of sin are death, but by the time taxes
are taken out, it's just sort of a tired feeling."
—Paula Poundstone

"Bad laws are the
worst sort of tyranny."
—Edmund Burke

Most laws are mandate
trials and fees.

Making a face is making a statement that can't be held against you in a court of law.

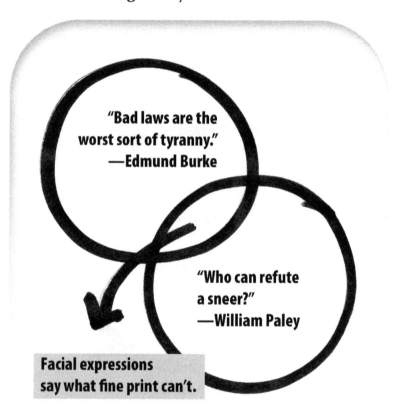

"Bad laws are the worst sort of tyranny."
—Edmund Burke

"Who can refute a sneer?"
—William Paley

Facial expressions say what fine print can't.

When kids can't talk back, they still find ways to communicate.

"Who can refute a sneer?"
—William Paley

Grown children are the best evaluators of their parents' parental skills.

"Parents wonder why the streams are bitter, when they themselves have poisoned the fountain."
—John Locke

**Spend more time with the people you want
to keep around.**

"Parents wonder why the
streams are bitter, when
they themselves have
poisoned the fountain."
—John Locke

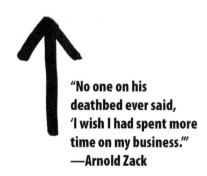

Ignore your kids and they'll return the favor.

"No one on his
deathbed ever said,
'I wish I had spent more
time on my business.'"
—Arnold Zack

We all do the best we can with
the time we have.

"No one on his
deathbed ever said,
'I wish I had spent
more time on
my business.'"
—Arnold Zack

Don't work so many late nights.

"Hindsight is always
twenty-twenty."
—Billy Wilder

More information leads to better decisions.

"Hindsight is always twenty-twenty."
—Billy Wilder

"I have seen the future; and it works."
—Lincoln Steffens

Hope means seeing the past as a sturdy foundation.

Con artists always make huge promises.

"I have seen the
future; and it works."
—Lincoln Steffens

"It was beautiful
and simple, as truly
great swindles are."
—O. Henry

Grand, sweeping
promises are either
declarations of
love or grifts.

We all want so badly to believe in what's too good to be true.

"It was beautiful and simple, as truly great swindles are."
—O. Henry

If only fairy godmothers bearing trust-funds were real.

"Zeal is very blind, or badly regulated, when it encroaches upon the rights of others."
—Pasquier Quesnel

Anyone evangelical about their cause
is selling it.

> "Zeal is very blind, or
> badly regulated, when
> it encroaches upon the
> rights of others."
> —Pasquier Quesnel

+

> "My imagination makes
> me human and makes me a
> fool; it gives me the world
> and exiles me from it."
> —Ursula K. Le Guin

It takes quite an imagination
to build a salable story.

**Fantasy stories make our world
more bearable.**

"My imagination makes me
human and makes me a fool;
it gives me the world and
exiles me from it."
—Ursula K. Le Guin

When reality gets too dour, we can
escape to dystopian fiction.

"If a free society cannot help
the many who are
poor, it cannot save the
few who are rich."
—John F. Kennedy

A free society has a price.

"If a free society cannot help the many who are poor, it cannot save the few who are rich."
—John F. Kennedy

If everyone were happy, nobody would be poor.

"Happiness is good health and a bad memory."
—Ingrid Bergman

Write down the things that should be celebrated.

"Happiness is good health and a bad memory."
—Ingrid Bergman

When good things are remembered, our society gets stronger.

"Unsung, the noblest deed will die."
—Pindar

To be praised for something, you have to do something.

"Unsung, the noblest deed will die."
—Pindar

To be remembered: do something for others and ignore the possible publicity.

"Millions long for immortality who don't know what to do with themselves on a rainy Sunday afternoon."
—Susan Ertz

Few plan to take over the world
in their downtime.

"Millions long for immortality
who don't know what to do
with themselves on a rainy
Sunday afternoon."
—Susan Ertz

Money, power, and fame take
a lot of time and effort.

"Money speaks in a language
all nations understand."
—Aphra Behn

How we spend our money is a moral issue.

"Money speaks in a language all nations understand."
—Aphra Behn

"Puritanism—the haunting fear that someone, somewhere, might be happy."
—H. L. Mencken

Every time we pay for conveniences, we buy indulgences.

Happiness and success bother
those without them.

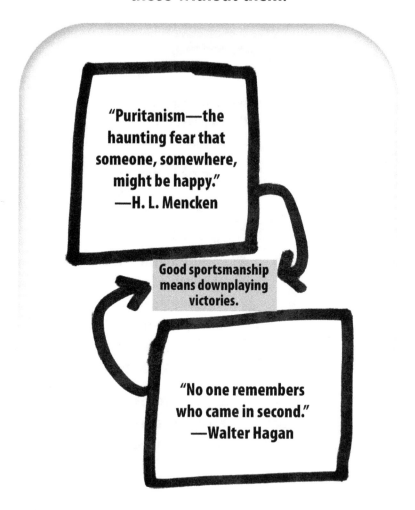

"Puritanism—the
haunting fear that
someone, somewhere,
might be happy."
—H. L. Mencken

Good sportsmanship
means downplaying
victories.

"No one remembers
who came in second."
—Walter Hagan

Billions of people never make the news.

"No one remembers
who came in second."
—Walter Hagan

**The stories you're not told are just
as important as the ones you embody.**

"To doubt everything or to believe
everything are two equally
convenient solutions; both dispense
with the necessity of reflection."
—Edgar Allen Poe

Inside every person are a thousand amazing stories.

"To doubt everything or to believe everything are two equally convenient solutions; both dispense with the necessity of reflection."
—Edgar Allen Poe

Everyone is far more complex that their obituary can ever state.

"Every murderer is probably somebody's old friend."
—Agatha Christie

People who absolutely love us or truly hate us don't have all the information.

"Every murderer is probably somebody's old friend."
—Agatha Christie

The enemy of your enemy is just another random person.

"Pay attention to your enemies, for they are the first to discover your mistakes."
—Antisthenes

Anyone who asks you to defend a harmless opinion is looking for trouble.

"Pay attention to your enemies, for they are the first to discover your mistakes."
—Antisthenes

"The difficult part in an argument is not to defend one's opinion but rather to know it."
—Andre Maurois

The best defense is avoiding unpromising confrontation.

How you see yourself in five years
is just a hypothesis.

"The difficult part in
an argument is not to
defend one's opinion
but rather to know it."
—Andre Maurois

Time takes hope and puts it to the scientific method.

"Science is an edged
tool with which men
play like children, and
cut their own fingers."
—Arthur S. Eddington

Controversy is not for the timid.

"Science is an edged tool with which men play like children, and cut their own fingers."
—Arthur S. Eddington

There's nothing braver than taking action on hard truth.

"Bravery never goes out of fashion."
—William Makepeace Thackery

It's not bravery if your knees don't
shake a little.

"Bravery never goes out of fashion."
—William Makepeace Thackery

Bravery is a form of optimism.

"Fear cannot be without hope
nor hope without fear."
—Benedict Spinoza

If you're rendered speechless, you need more time to find your words. It's not that they aren't there.

"Fear cannot be without hope nor hope without fear."
—Benedict Spinoza

Silence expresses shock.

"What we cannot speak we must pass over in silence."
—Ludwig Wittgenstein

Most artists are known for work
they consider minor.

"What we cannot speak we
must pass over in silence."
—Ludwig Wittgenstein

You have very little say on
how you're interpreted, so
be as articulate as possible.

"The worst tragedy for a poet
is to be admired through
being misunderstood."
—Jean Cocteau

**To recall a dark event in a fine light
is an act of closure.**

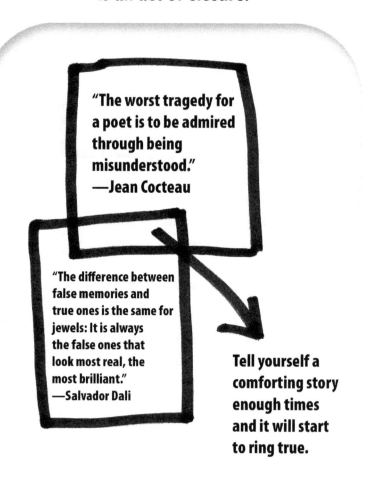

"The worst tragedy for a poet is to be admired through being misunderstood."
—Jean Cocteau

"The difference between false memories and true ones is the same for jewels: It is always the false ones that look most real, the most brilliant."
—Salvador Dali

Tell yourself a comforting story enough times and it will start to ring true.

All advice is given through a lens of survivorship.

"The difference between false memories and true ones is the same for jewels: It is always the false ones that look most real, the most brilliant."
—Salvador Dali

Take the word of rich people with a fistful of salt.

"Earn enough money so you can afford to waste time."
—Kiyosa Sagawa

Money can't purchase happiness
but it can erase a lot of worry.

"Earn enough money so you
can afford to waste time."
—Kiyosa Sagawa

Money is a tool not a magic trick.

"Money is a terrible master
but an excellent servant."
—P.T. Barnum

Executioners are never paid enough.

"Money is a terrible master
but an excellent servant."
—P.T. Barnum

The work you need to do
should earn a higher wage.

"Hanging was the worst
use a man could be put to."
—Sir Henry Wotton

December 15

A quick death is the best kind.

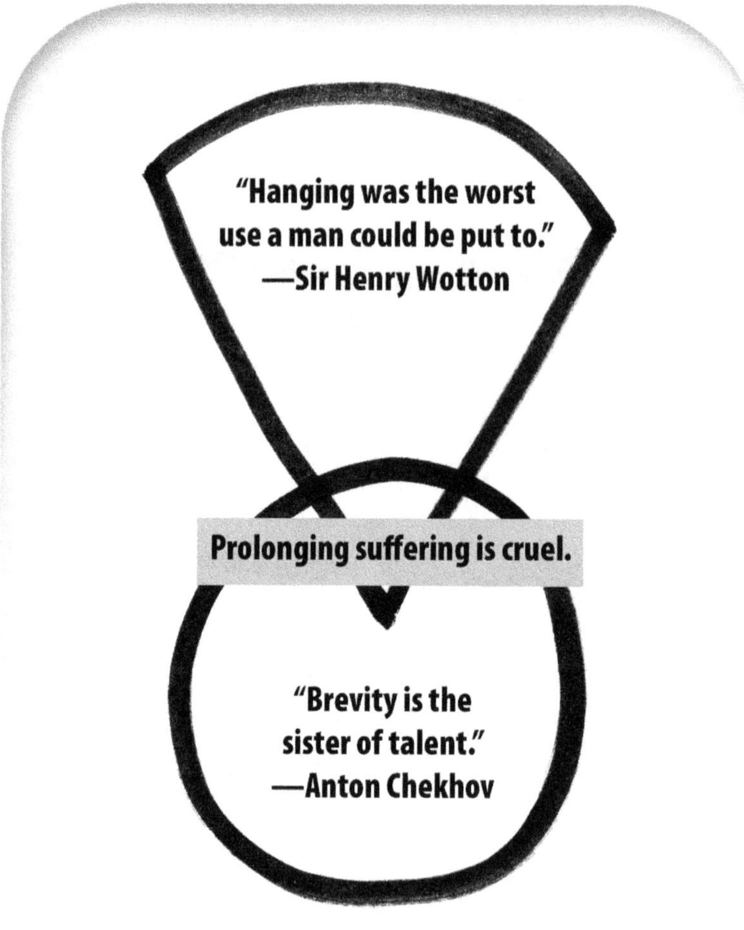
"Hanging was the worst use a man could be put to."
—Sir Henry Wotton
Prolonging suffering is cruel.
"Brevity is the sister of talent."
—Anton Chekhov

Eternity is a surprisingly short word.

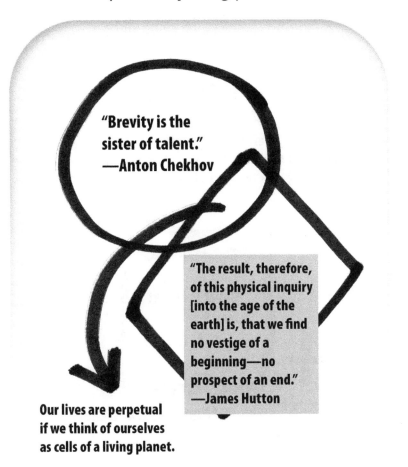

"Brevity is the
sister of talent."
—Anton Chekhov

"The result, therefore,
of this physical inquiry
[into the age of the
earth] is, that we find
no vestige of a
beginning—no
prospect of an end."
—James Hutton

Our lives are perpetual
if we think of ourselves
as cells of a living planet.

If you wish something miraculous would happen, it either has or will.

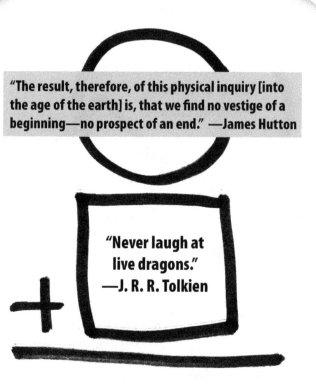

"The result, therefore, of this physical inquiry [into the age of the earth] is, that we find no vestige of a beginning—no prospect of an end." —James Hutton

"Never laugh at live dragons." —J. R. R. Tolkien

With enough time absolutely anything is possible.

A master of any field has a whiff of the magical about her.

"Never laugh at
live dragons."
—J. R. R. Tolkien

Imagination is key to innovation.

"Politics is the art of the possible."
—Otto von Bismarck

Never forget who your audience is.

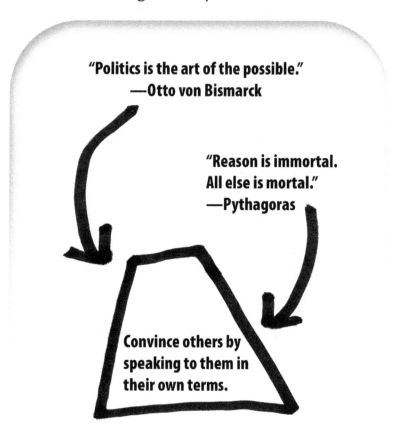

"Politics is the art of the possible."
—Otto von Bismarck

"Reason is immortal.
All else is mortal."
—Pythagoras

Convince others by
speaking to them in
their own terms.

The less of a future you have, the less you want to think about it.

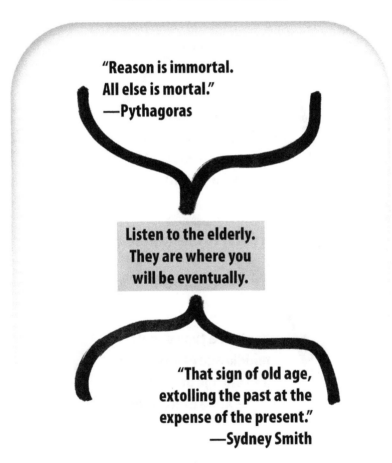

"Reason is immortal.
All else is mortal."
—Pythagoras

Listen to the elderly.
They are where you
will be eventually.

"That sign of old age,
extolling the past at the
expense of the present."
—Sydney Smith

Time alters memory.

"That sign of old age, extolling the past at the expense of the present."
—Sydney Smith

It's never to late to peak.

"Youth is a time of getting, middle age of improving, and old age of spending."
—Anne Bradstreet

A youthful person strives.

"Youth is a time of getting, middle age of improving, and old age of spending."
—Anne Bradstreet

To rebel against mortality: set lofty goals at any age.

"We are but dust and shadow."
—Horace

All of this is temporary.

"We are but dust
and shadow."
—Horace

Change is
relentless and
inescapable.

"Time takes
and gives all."
—Giordano Bruno

We only borrow everything
we think we own.

"Time takes and gives all."
—Giordano Bruno

We are stewards, not owners, of
everything on our planet.

"No man can lose
what he never had."
—Izaak Walton

The richer we get, the stupider
the things we lust after.

"No man can lose what he never had."
—Izaak Walton

To envy is to feel loss for
things never acquired.

"Excess of wealth is cause of covetousness."
—Christopher Marlowe

One greedy mistake can be corrected, a string of them signals a flawed mindset.

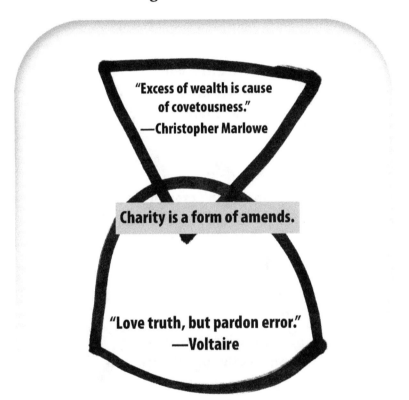

"Excess of wealth is cause of covetousness."
—Christopher Marlowe

Charity is a form of amends.

"Love truth, but pardon error."
—Voltaire

Knowing right from wrong is not even the half of it.

"Love truth, but pardon error."
—Voltaire

Truth that doesn't prompt change might as well be gibberish.

"Truth is a torch that gleams through the fog without dispelling it."
—Claude Adrien Helvétius

A truth stated plainly can still be interpreted in opposing ways.

"Truth is a torch that gleams through the fog without dispelling it."
—Claude Adrien Helvétius

Listen closely for spin in your own voice.

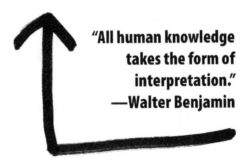

"All human knowledge takes the form of interpretation."
—Walter Benjamin

It's more interesting to listen instead of just waiting to talk.

"All human knowledge takes the form of interpretation."
—Walter Benjamin

"There is no such thing as conversation. There are interesting monologues, that is all."
—Rebecca West

Everyone involved in a conversation has an agenda.

Everything references everything else.

"There is no such thing as conversation. There are interesting monologues, that is all."
—Rebecca West

+

"When we try to pick out anything by itself we find that it is bound fast by a thousand invisible cords that cannot be broken, to everything in the universe."
—John Muir

You are the result of a billion different events.

One small change can ripple across the world.

"When we try to pick out anything by itself we find that it is bound fast by a thousand invisible cords that cannot be broken, to everything in the universe."
—John Muir

"My friends, love is better than anger. Hope is better than fear. Optimism is better than despair. So let us be loving, hopeful and optimistic. And we'll change the world."
—Jack Layton (WIKI)

You have so much more potential than you realize.

About the
Author

Jessica Hagy is an artist and writer best known for her Webby award-winning webcomic, *Indexed* (www.thisisindexed.com) and is the author of the nonfiction books, *The Art of War Visualized, How to Be Interesting,* and *Indexed*. A fixture in the creative online space, Jessica has been prolifically illustrating, consulting, and speaking internationally since 2006. Her work has been described as "deceptively simple," "undeniably brilliant," and "our favorite reason for the Internet to exist." She mixes data (both quantitative and qualitative) with humor, insight, and simple visuals to make even the most complex concepts immediately accessible and relevant. Her work has been flatteringly featured in *Wired, The New York Times, Harvard Business Review,* and *Forbes,* among many others. Her work has been translated into more than a dozen languages. Jessica lives in Seattle, Washington.

CPSIA information can be obtained
at www.ICGtesting.com
Printed in the USA
LVHW031056111219
640004LV00023B/652/P